*Sniper Ace*

Bruno Sutkus in the early autumn of 1944 in the Carpathian mountains. He carries the 98k carbine with Korntunnel sight fitment. The optic is the Ajak telescopic sight with four-fold magnification on the low swivel mounting. The binocular is a 6 x 30. He wears a brown sniper jacket with a hood.

# ~ SNIPER ACE ~

## FROM THE EASTERN FRONT TO SIBERIA

*Bruno Sutkus*

*The Autobiography of a Wehrmacht Sniper*

~

*Introduction by David L. Robbins*

*Translation by Geoffrey Brooks*

Frontline Books, London

*Sniper Ace*

This edition published in 2009 by Frontline Books,
an imprint of Pen & Sword Books Ltd,
47 Church Street, Barnsley, S. Yorkshire, S70 2AS

www.frontline-books.com

Copyright © Munin Verlag GmbH, 2003
Translation © Pen & Sword Books Limited, 2009
This edition © Pen & Sword Books Limited, 2009
Introduction © David L. Robbins, 2009

ISBN: 978-1-84832-548-7

Frontline Books and Munin Verlag both wish to express their gratitude to
Martin Benz for his major contribution to the production of the German- and
English-language editions of this book.

PUBLISHING HISTORY
*Im Fadenkreuz: Tagebuch eines Scharfschützen* was originally published by
Munin Verlag in 2003. This is the first English-language edition of the text
and includes a new introduction by David L. Robbins.

*CIP data records for this title are available from the British Library*

For more information on our books, please visit
www.frontline-books.com, email info@frontline-books.com
or write to us at the above address.

Typeset by JCS Publishing Services Ltd, www.jcs-publishing.co.uk

Maps drawn by Red Lion Prints

Printed in the UK by the MPG Books Group

~

# *Contents*

~

# Illustrations and Maps

# ~ Maps ~

THE JOURNEY OF
BRUNO SUTKUS

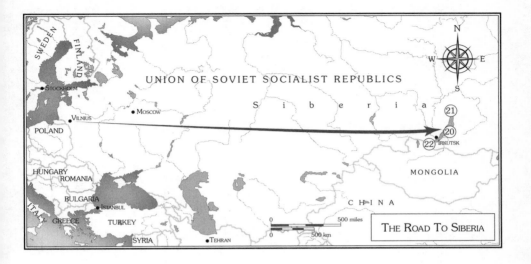

UNION OF SOVIET SOCIALIST REPUBLICS

S i b e r i a

SWEDEN
FINLAND
STOCKHOLM
VILNIUS
MOSCOW
POLAND
HUNGARY
ROMANIA
BULGARIA
ISTANBUL
ITALY GREECE
TURKEY
SYRIA
TEHRAN
IRKUTSK
MONGOLIA
C H I N A

21
20
22

0       500 miles
0       500 km

THE ROAD TO SIBERIA

N
W    E
S

## The Journey of Bruno Sutkus: 1943–1997

1  Gumbinnen, East Prussia
2  Vilnius, Lithuania
3  Debica, Poland
4  Tarnopol, Poland
5  Meseritz, Germany
6  Lemberg, Ukraine
7  Slobodka-Lesna, Ukraine
8  Beskid mountain range
9  Kruzlova, Czechoslovakia
10 Gleiwitz, Poland
11 Burgstädt, Germany
12 Stöbnich, Germany

13 Brest-Litovsk, Poland
14 Leipzig, Germany
15 Vilnius, Lithuania
16 Fichtenhöhe, Germany
17 Gumbinnen, East Prussia
18 Leketschai, Lithuania
19 Irkutsk, Siberia
20 Rudovka, Siberia
21 Sherenkov, Siberia
22 Vilnius, Lithuania
23 Berlin, Germany

Map 1 (opposite page) shows the country borders as they stood in 1943; map 2 (above) shows the de facto borders of 1945.

~

# *Introduction*

I have not been to war.

The closest I have come to combat is to speak with hundreds of soldiers and veterans, stand on dozens of battlefields, study war closely through written records and recollections. My experiences of battle are all vicarious.

As such, the argument could be made that I am not qualified to write an introduction for a book detailing the life and sacrifices of a warrior. I accept this, and because I do, drive myself even more in my profession as a novelist, largely of Second World War tales, to be as informed and authentic in my portrayals as I can humanly be.

And there lies my qualification to pen this introduction. These pages, written by the late Bruno Sutkus, detail a life of misery and courage, of death-dealing and survival, that no one but he could have withstood. By its nature, this memoir, *because* it is so singular, reduces us all to the role of vicarious passengers, voyeurs in Sutkus's painful past. I will state without fear of contradiction that neither you nor I, though we may be among the most experienced or hardy of people, could have done what Sutkus describes. Here, in this world of other people's lives, I am a master.

When the publishers of *Sniper Ace* asked that I craft an introduction, I became hesitant when I learnt Sutkus was a member of the Nazi Hitler Youth. Nonetheless, I pressed on reading the manuscript, to see if it might intrigue me enough to carry me past my reluctance. What I discovered was a story that beggared the imagination for calculated killing on the Eastern Front, and the intimate details of doing such a thing. The book follows Sutkus from his first days in battle, interspersed with excerpts from his actual sniper's field diary, to his inevitable imprisonment and exile at the hands of the communists in Siberia. At war's end, the feared assassin became a forced-labour slave on Soviet collective farms. The mercy he could not show to the hundreds of enemies who fell under his crosshairs was in turn denied him by the Soviets who kept him from his homeland for fifty-two years.

As a young soldier, Bruno Sutkus threw himself into his role as reaper of Russian lives, and his telling is commensurately grim. His prose is as sharp as his sniper scope. He explains how 'accuracy guaranteed my life', and 'only the strong and lucky man survives'. Sutkus – any man – could do this only by believing his own life was forfeit. He says: 'I never thought for a moment that I should spend all my Wehrmacht service in the most advanced positions and still emerge alive at the end of it.'

In the end, I did not forgive Sutkus his childhood foray in the Nazi Party because forgiveness was not required in order to be amazed at the rest of his life. The author suffered the worst of humanity over decades – even meted out his own share of it during the war – but never lost his guts, and not once during his long banishment did he waiver in his desire to return to his homeland. In so doing, he found love, a family and regained, in my eyes, his honour.

You will see, as I did, that *Sniper Ace* is larger than a sniper's story, though that may be its initial appeal. It is, in the final analysis, a grand and moving account of willpower, duty, redemption and the limits of human endurance.

*David L. Robbins*
*Richmond, Virginia*
*USA*
*June 2009*

~

# *Preface*

I was a Wehrmacht sniper and this is my first-hand account. It was my task to root out enemy snipers and perform other tasks of that kind. Additionally I was seconded to various company commanders for objectives they had in mind. To be a sniper in the foremost trench on the front line, or in No Man's Land ahead of it, was a dangerous assignment. A lot was expected of a sniper. I carried out my superior officers' orders: the lives of comrades often depended on my doing so precisely.

Generally speaking the sniper did not search out his victim but was placed in the front sector where it was necessary to remove one or more specified opponents. An observer was appointed to assist the sniper and confirm any claims. These claims would be recorded in the sniper's log and in my case were authenticated by the battalion adjutant.

In this manner I helped my comrades repel many Soviet attacks. At the front the rules of civilised society do not exist, only the rules of war. I came through all its horrors, and saw and experienced very many things I am unable to forget. Although decades have passed, I still wake up in a sweat from time to time, having dreamt that I am back at the front. The war left a negative shadow in people's hearts, and the modern generation cannot begin to conceive what the soldier at the front had to endure.

*Bruno Sutkus*

~

# Publisher's Foreword
## (from the original German edition)

The log kept by Bruno Sutkus during the Second World War is the basis for this book. The log contains the notes he kept of each of his claimed successes as a sniper. They are authenticated and thus make a unique contribution to the history of the Second World War. His claim is 209 hits on enemy personnel, and there can be no doubt as to the veracity of this figure. Sutkus spent only six months on the Eastern Front. In view of this short period of activity, he must count as one of the most successful snipers of the German Wehrmacht.

His actual successes may be greater. He obtained no confirmation of earlier claims and his log does not begin until 2 July 1944. It contains entries for 12 and 13 July 1944 where five claims lack confirmation. Together with the Iron Cross 1. and 2. Class, Sutkus was awarded the rare Sniper Proficiency Badge in the highest grade, and, though only a private soldier, was mentioned in the *Wehrmacht Report*.

This book is not intended to portray the fighting in which Grenadier Regiment 196 was involved, but rather describes the experience of infantry warfare ahead of the front lines as seen through the eyes of a sniper. After a period on the run in Lithuania pursued by the Soviets, the author was caught, suffered torture and was banished for life to Siberia. Here he survived the worst degradation and harsh labour, escaping death on several occasions at the hands of a brutal and merciless regime and resisted all Soviet lures aimed at recruiting him to spy for them in West Germany. He was held captive by the Soviets for decades. Only after the fall of the communist system did he manage to return to Germany. This book is the unique, engrossing and tragic story of a German infantryman of the Second World War.

# ~ PART ONE ~

# 1

## *Childhood in East Prussia*

I was born on 14 May 1924 at Tannenwalde in the Schlossberg district of East Prussia. In 1928 my parents, modest field labourers on the estate of Arno Braemer, moved from Tannenwalde to Fichtenhöhe. This village was right on the border with Lithuania. The Scheschuppe River was the frontier: this side was Germany, the other bank was Lithuania.

When I was born in East Prussia, my Lithuanian parents failed to register my birth in Lithuania, which would have given me Lithuanian nationality. My birth was registered at Schillfelde/ Schlossberg in Germany, but under German family law, because my father was not German, I was not entitled to German nationality automatically on the basis of having been born in East Prussia. Thus I grew up as a stateless person in the German Reich. My father was the unwanted, illegitimate son of a member of the aristocracy, which further complicated matters.

Fichtenhöhe was my home town and I was very much attached to it. In early childhood my parents gave me jobs to do that were within my youthful capabilities. I was given sole charge of forty rabbits and had to collect hay and feed the animals. Since my mother worked daily in the field, I had other tasks to perform for the household, including obtaining hay and grass for the ducks and geese and tending the pigs. At harvest time in summer we youngsters were called upon to drive the rig with its team of four horses or follow with the raking machine to keep losses of corn and ears to a minimum.

The reaping was done in fine weather. The boys would be given work in the barns. Beforehand, the farms inspector would request the village schoolmaster to release a number of boys from lessons in order to help with the harvest. We would then head out joyfully to the work. It was better than being in school where our teacher Visarius, a Hauptmann in the Reserve, was ruthless in his zeal and, upon detecting the least inattention, would apply his hazel rod to the buttocks of the offender. Needless to say, the classroom was always as silent as a tomb. Visarius taught us national pride. Often I failed to do my homework, and while the other children would be allowed home, I had to remain behind to complete it. Only when my teacher was satisfied with my effort would he permit me to go. I was the butt of the other boys' teasing and was often set upon. Being small in build I often came off worst and would arrive home in tears, where my mother would tenderly dry my face. Later when I grew a bit, I got my revenge with interest.

I liked helping out with the harvesting. I earnt eighty pfennigs daily for work on the farm. Sometimes I would be due as much as ten Reichsmarks and be paid out after signing the payroll. With great pride I would hand over my earnings to my mother. She opened a savings account for me and helped me put a little aside. In summertime, when berries and mushrooms were ready to pick, my father would take me to the woods to gather baskets of them. I liked fishing the Scheschuppe River best. It had a lot of fish. I used to set a long line baited with worms overnight and find large pike and eels on the hooks next morning. I would then sell them to Glanert, who ran the inn at Moosbach. I also had income from the berries and mushrooms.

We used to sell the geese or pigs in the autumn. My mother invested some of the proceeds into my savings book. By the time I was called up for military service in 1943 I had 1,238 Reichsmarks saved up from my farm work. I have kept the book as a souvenir. When we boys were ten we had to join the *Jungvolk*. My mother bought my uniform, of which I was very proud, from the money in my account. At this age, every autumn I worked for a farmer at Fichtenhöhe lifting potatoes, which paid one Reichsmark daily. He gave us five meals a day. In the evening we would pick apples and pears from his orchard and take them home. Later, when the war came and many of the young men were conscripted, the farmers' wives were always asking us to help out at harvest time. After working throughout the day on the farm, we would then spend the evening and night until three the next morning helping the farmer scythe the corn. The girls bound the sheaves and set them up for drying. This work paid five Reichsmarks. Additionally the farmer's wife would treat us to a celebration and once there was even some schnaps. Finally we sang our way home to sleep at around four.

After the eighth grade at state school I left in March 1938 at the age of fourteen. At this age we had to leave the *Jungvolk* and join the Hitler Youth (*Hitler Jugend*). I would now clash occasionally with my mother. Every Sunday I had to go to Schirwindt with the Hitler Youth. My mother wanted me to attend Catholic Mass at Schillfelde Church, but I never had the time because of my duties with the Hitler Youth, where I was soon promoted to Scharführer (squad leader).

From then until 1940 I became apprenticed on the farm of Arno Braemer. There was a shortage of farmhands because so many men were being conscripted. As a result I was soon trained in all essential aspects of farm work. At about this time my father fell ill, and Herr Braemer asked me to fill in for my father in return for payment in kind. I was given four horses to care for. I had to get up very early to clean and feed them. Because I did not get much sleep, my mother often found me in a semi-stupor in the mornings. I was overtired from labouring eleven hours a day with the team, harrowing or ploughing, sowing or harvesting. During my childhood I was no 'Mummy's boy', but became hardened from early on to hard work, so that later the effort required of me at the front by the Wehrmacht was much easier for me to bear than for others.

In 1940 I was granted a Foreigner's Identity Card by the Third Reich. This document granted me the right to live in Schlossberg as a stateless person. In 1941 my application for German nationality by naturalisation was approved and I received a certificate showing my domicile as Fichtenhöhe/Schlossberg. For the first time in my life I had official proof of my date of birth in a document. I submitted a copy to the Wehrmacht recruiting office at Gumbinnen and was conscripted a couple of years later. I retained the Foreigner's Identity Card, since I was not obliged to surrender it.

On 22 June 1941 war broke out between the German Reich and the Soviet Union. Since we lived on the frontier we could watch the Wehrmacht troops crossing the Scheschuppe into Lithuania. The Soviet occupiers were forced out and fled back to where they belonged, but the frontier between Germany and Lithuania continued to be guarded and had many border posts. As I knew the area well it was no problem for me to cross over whenever I wanted, although some caution was necessary, and one had to keep a good lookout near where the border guards were stationed or might be hiding under camouflage. I loved nature and had learnt how to observe it. This made it easy for me to spot the border guards.

The Lithuanians on the other side of the river could not get things such as lighters, flints, pumice stone and so on, and these were much in demand. I used to buy them in Schirwindt or Schillfelde and smuggle them into Lithuania, where I would exchange them for hams, sausage, butter and geese, and so on, things which were only available in limited supply in Germany once rationing was introduced. I would cross the border river around midnight, careful not to be caught by the customs officials. I could literally hear my heartbeat. I had learnt early on to control my fear and above all memorise the terrain exactly. That was the best pre-military training on the road to becoming a sniper, for whom it was so important to read the terrain and where the least inattention to detail could cost your life.

Eighteen-year-olds – I celebrated my eighteenth birthday on 14 May 1942 – were transferred with great ceremony from the Hitler Youth into the Sturmabteilung (SA). Since we were at war, men of the SA-Wehrmannschaften were given military training. I was liable for call-up into the German Wehrmacht (Armed Forces) in 1942. However, one very hot day I drank some bitterly cold water; the result was double pneumonia. My employer requested a year's postponement for me at the Wehrmacht induction office, which was granted. My military training continued in the SA. In the shooting competition I got a high score, which came to the attention of Sturmführer Sommer – I was considered a marksman. I was given a small-calibre rifle and plenty of ammunition to take home for practice. In my spare time I shot at sparrows, which were very numerous in our neighbourhood. These sparrows grew so wary that it seemed they divined my intentions and would take flight when they spotted me. I had to creep up on them very stealthily to get off a successful shot. Small crows were even more circumspect, but practice makes perfect, and I soon became successful.

# 2

## *I Become a Soldier*

In July 1943 the postman brought my call-up papers directly to the field where I was working. I, at once, unhitched the team and rode back to the farmhouse. That was my last working day at Gut Fichtenhöhe. Next morning my parents accompanied me to the small railway station at Doristal where we said our farewells. My mother told me, 'Bruno, do not forget God, and then He will not forget you. I will pray to Him every day and night for your life, which is now in His hands. I know that you must be a soldier and can change nothing. Do only what is your duty, for the enemy soldier has a mother and wife too, and perhaps children waiting at home for him to come back, just like I shall be.' I boarded the train and kissed my dear little mother goodbye, not knowing whether it might be for the last time. The farewell was very difficult for her – I was her only son. The train steamed off into uncertainty.

On 22 July 1943 I reported to Füsilier-Ersatz Batallion 22 at Gumbinnen in East Prussia and began my life as a soldier. I did not like the exercises and drill. At Gumbinnen I swore my oath of allegiance to the Führer, Adolf Hitler. In the second week we fired live ammunition. Five rounds were issued to each man and we had to aim them at a circular target with twelve concentric rings. It was the first time we had used our rifles. My first round was low and hit ring ten. I raised the rifle a little and got an eleven next time. I scored twelve with the last three. The battalion commander happened to be passing and saw my results. He had me issued with another five rounds to repeat the test. This time I got twelve with all five. He asked where I had learnt to shoot. I told him about the SA-Wehrmannschaft where I had fulfilled all the requirements and been awarded the SA military proficiency badge.

Two weeks after my induction I was given seven days' special leave on account of my marksmanship and became the envy of my colleagues. I was given a ride home in an army vehicle because Fichtenhöhe was not far from Gumbinnen.

At the end of July 1943 we boarded camouflaged railway goods wagons and headed by night to the field-training battalion in Russia for further training. This we received during the day, for at night we had to guard the Minsk–Orsha railway line, a favourite target for partisans. Once I fell asleep on sentry duty. When I woke up my rifle was gone; the duty sergeant had confiscated it. I was handed over to the guard commander and locked in a cell. I felt ashamed. At midday I was escorted to the company office by the duty NCO and two privates wearing sidearms. Oberleutnant Braun explained how serious a matter it was to fall asleep on guard and the dangers that it could give lead to. He decided to let me off with a warning this time but I had to scrub the corridor as a punishment.

On the training company's first session with live rounds I excelled in the presence of Oberleutnant Braun and the battalion CO. At one hundred metres on the twelve-ring target I scored four twelves and an eleven. Next I had to fire five rounds at a camouflaged target and scored three twelves and two elevens. I did not stay long in the training company. After a month or so I was drafted to the Sniper School at Vilnius in Lithuania. The school was located in a barracks near the St Peter and Paul Church. The same complex housed an officers' training establishment. Our course lasted from 1 August to the end of December 1943.

We were shown captured Russian film from which we gained an idea of the things a sniper had to master, especially fieldcraft, concealment, marksmanship (of course) and range estimation. Over these five months we learnt to absorb all the minute details a sniper had to bear in mind in order to spot the enemy hidden in the natural environment and to avoid being picked out himself. The instructors were good. In the countryside they taught us how to recognise a target, pass information, estimate range and shoot at moving targets. I developed great accuracy in the latter. I realised that in those five months I had to absorb what I could in order to survive in the field. At the end of the course all those who qualified received the most modern sniper's rifle with telescopic sight, binoculars and a camouflage jacket (*tarnjacke*). I was given a certificate confirming that I had passed out from sniper school and was warned never to allow another person to handle my rifle.

At the beginning of January 1944 I returned to the field-training battalion at Kolomea, not far from the Minsk–Orsha railway line. Excitement reigned, for our unit was in the process of entraining. The battalion was to be absorbed into Grenadier Regiment 196 of 68. *Berlin-Brandenburgische* Infantry Division, presently being reformed at Debica training depot near Cracow. We had to go right across Poland and were held up on many occasions waiting for the tracks to be repaired after partisans blew them up.

At Debica we were assigned to our new units. I was to be attached to II Batallion/Gren Regt 196 as a sniper. I got another twenty-one days' special leave to start off with and went home. All too soon the time was up and, once back with my unit, we were clanking off again to join up with 68. Infantry Division at Tarnopol, where there was heavy fighting. Our train came to a halt outside Tarnopol because Russian tanks had broken through our front lines and encircled the town. Divisional HQ ordered our battalion back to Meseritz training depot near Frankfurt an der Oder to await further orders. 68. *Berlin-Brandenburgische* Infantry Division was made up of Grenadier Regiments 169, 188 and 196, Artillery Regiment 168, Reconnaissance Unit 168, Anti-tank Unit 168 and other logistics groups operating together in the usual infantry-division arrangement of the time. When the Russian campaign started in June 1941, the division was in the east and took part in the fighting around Tcherkassy, Poltava and Kharkov. In the first six months of 1942 it fought near Isyum; from autumn 1942 to the beginning of 1943 at Voronezh; in the spring that year within the encirclement at Oboyan and Sumy; and in the summer offensive at Kursk.

In the winter of 1943 the division fought alongside 1. SS Panzer Division *Leibstandarte Adolf Hitler* at Kiev, Zhitomir and Radomyshl. In February and March 1944 the division was reformed at Demba training depot. A battlegroup was sent from there to fight at Kovel. While we were standing by at Meseritz on the Oder, a major part of 68. Inf Div was involved in the incessant fighting at Tarnopol, where it was surrounded and suffered enormous losses, though able eventually to break out. All this led to 68. Inf Div being reformed. I was ordered to report to II Battalion Staff/Grenadier Regiment 196.

We set out for the front, where we were to relieve a Hungarian unit that had been involved in heavy fighting and severely mauled in the western Ukraine. We reached the assembly point in the afternoon and camouflaged up to avoid being spotted prematurely by enemy air reconnaissance. We were in the Lemberg area, where 68. Infantry Division formed part of 1st Hungarian Army. Finally it was the real thing, and I trembled at the sound of battle, the thunder of the heavy guns and the rattle of machine-gun fire. Once it grew dark we went forward, passing a burning Soviet tank that had got through our lines and been hit by a *Panzerfaust*. It stank of burning flesh. Dead Germans, Russians and Hungarians were strewn all around. The corpses had lain some time in the sun, and were bloated, black and decomposing. We relieved the Hungarians, who left their dead where they lay.

The enemy had noticed activity in our sector and shelled the trenches. Very close by was a farm where we set up a mortar in the centre of the courtyard. During a pause while the crew was taking refreshment a shell exploded amongst them, decapitating one and ripping another open from chest to abdomen. We had occupied the sector two hours and already had two men dead. It occurred to me that I should cover over the corpses with straw, but then I began to tremble and got away from the scene as quick as decently possible.

At 1000 hrs the artillery fire stopped and the Soviets attacked with tanks and infantry. This was a local probe, searching for the weak spots in our front line. Many of our men began to fire at a range of 500 to 600 metres, mostly from anxiety. One had to wait until the enemy came within 200 metres to expect any success. I had overcome my own fears much earlier. Naturally I reflected on dying and recalled my mother's parting words not to kill, but only to do my duty. This was all very well, but now we were soldiers and had no choice but to shoot. It was either them or me!

Amongst the Soviet infantry I saw an officer of Asian appearance driving his men forward towards our trenches with pistol drawn. I shot him down. I kept firing. Each round was a hit. The infantry was forced to seek some cover. Anyone who stood up and attempted to advance was hit. The commissars remained behind their soldiers, herding them forwards into our defensive fire. I aimed first at the commissars and shot them all down. When the leading ranks of infantry noticed that the commissars were out of it they turned and went back to their own lines The attack on our sector had been warded off.

Next the enemy tanks and infantry attacked our neighbouring company. We concentrated fire on the Russian infantry to separate them from the tanks, for the combination of infantry and these steel colossi was greatly feared. Before the attack I had an issue of 120 rounds. Now I had to request a fresh supply. My expenditure during the attack was not logged. While it was under way I noticed that many of our men had set their rifle sights for 600 metres initially and forgotten to adjust it to 100 metres as the enemy closed in.

At first my presence in the ranks as a sniper was hardly noticed. Only when it began to be realised what a sniper could achieve and how much depended upon him did the opinion of my comrades change. The enemy had certainly noticed that a sniper was operating in the sector of the front directly opposite them, for now they moved about more cautiously. I could have taken out quite a few more of them but was anxious not to betray my position. First I took a very good look at the terrain and estimated the distances. No Man's Land was about 500 metres wide. There was a Russian sniper ahead of their trenches and well camouflaged. He had a good view of our lines and had inflicted losses on our men. Their trenches had an 'Ivan' every ten to fifteen metres. We had fifty to seventy metres between each grenadier. Our casualties were not replaced, so our trenches became gradually less populated. Nevertheless the front line had to be held at all costs.

# 3

## *My First Fifty-Two Successes as a Sniper*

We were dug in at Slobodka-Lesna. As 8 May 1944 dawned I swept the terrain to the east through the telescopic sight of my weapon. Three hundred metres ahead, exactly where I had spotted an enemy sniper's hiding place, I could see clearly the impressions of his boots in the grass where he had vacated and then reoccupied his position. To create his lair he had done some spadework, removing some sods of turf to make a depression in which to bed himself behind his rifle. He wore a camouflage jacket and mask. Some way to the right was a rise with some rubble where a house had probably stood. This location attracted me like a magnet, and I kept checking the position of the sun in relation to it. Around noon I noticed a flash and some movement. In the ruined cellar was a Russian artillery-spotter's post. Using the scissors-periscope they had a good view of our trenches and could direct their fire accurately. Upon further observation I detected a camouflage net that made a slight movement. At one place the communication trench had been dug too shallowly, was poorly camouflaged and accordingly could be seen easily. I watched the Russians entering the cellar. At 500 metres two men – senior officers by their uniforms – came through the communication trench. I shot one down. The other reacted with shock and held his ground. I had already reloaded and shot him too.

The Russian sniper I had detected earlier identified my position from these two rounds. He made a slight turn to fire at me and I hit him at the same instant as his bullet hissed past my head. I had begun my sniper log (*Scharfschützenheft*) on 2 July 1944, and was credited on this day with one confirmed claim (*1*).

---

CLAIM NO: *1*
DATE: *8.5.1944*
PLACE: *Slobodka-Lesna, Sector 6./Gren Regt 196*
EVENT: *S[utkus] was ordered to engage enemy snipers near Slobodka-Lesna and put one sniper out of action. Range 600 metres.*
WITNESSED BY: *Lt Walter, Battalion Adjutant*

On 9 May 1944 at Slobodka-Lesna, 7./Gren Regt 196 was receiving very accurate mortar fire. I found it difficult to make out the Russian trench. I climbed a tree and saw at 300 metres distance a well-prepared and fortified Russian position with a large number of troops present. I saw tanks and anti-tank guns. Patiently I waited for a Russian officer to show himself. The long wait was successful: as a well-dressed Russian made his way along the trench I shot him down (2) and shortly afterwards another (3).

CLAIM NO: *2*
DATE: *9.5.1944*
PLACE: *Slobodka-Lesna, Sector 7./Gren Regt 196*
EVENT: *S. was ordered to engage enemy mortar team and put one Russian out of action. Range 300 m.*
WITNESSED BY: *Lt Walter, Bn Adj*

The Russians returned fire at my tree and I was unable to get down for some time. My observer, Battalion adjutant Walter, confirmed the two claims and I was able to inform both 7. Company and II Batallion of the expected direction of the coming attack. I was then wounded by a mortar splinter and temporarily put out of action myself. I returned to duty at the front on 2 July 1944.

From my position on the left flank of 7./Gren Regt 196 on the road from Slobodka-Lesna to Chlobiczyn-Lesny, around 2030 hrs, from 250 metres range I shot a Russian soldier digging a trench (4). The witness was Uffz (Unteroffizier) Hoffmann.

On the same stretch of road on 3 July 1944 I was ordered to cooperate with 5. Company/Gren Regt 196, from whose positions it was thought I would be afforded a better view of the enemy lines. The enemy was holding out in woodland from where they made numerous local sorties aimed at forcing our troops to abandon their trenches. I could not find a favourable place from where to see the enemy positions and had to climb a tree. After waiting patiently, at 1900 two well-dressed Russian officers appeared, apparently on a tour of inspection. They stood around for a moment, giving orders and pointing to their map. At 600 metres I fired and hit one of the officers in the chest (5). The second had not recovered from the shock before my next shot hit him, also in the chest (6). I jumped down from the tree in great haste to elude the hurricane of fire from mortars and infantry weapons aimed at my perch.

CLAIM NOS: *5 and 6*
DATE: *3.7.1944*
PLACE: *Slobodka-Lesna towards Chlobiczyn-Lesny, Sector 5./Gren Regt 196*
EVENT: *S. was sent from the right flank of 5. Company trenches to engage the enemy in the Poharz woods. S. shot two Russians in the chest from great range in the Poharz glade. (5) Time 1900 hrs. Range 600 metres. (6) Time 1930 hrs Range 500m*
WITNESS: *Gefr Küller*

The next day they bombarded us with propaganda through loudspeakers, something like: 'German soldiers, lay down your weapons, you have lost the war. We guarantee you your lives and your return home afterwards.' They were not so kindly towards me, addressing me as 'a bloodthirsty Fascist who can expect no mercy'. It was obvious that I was getting on their nerves, for they called up one sniper after another to winkle me out. I could always sense, however, where they had concealed themselves. I could literally feel it when I was in their sights. Undoubtedly there would only have been some minor matter of final adjustment preventing their firing and finishing me off. I was often shown a lure but never fell for one. Now and then they would raise a mannequin in officer's uniform. It had a lifeless face and so I was not deceived. Sometimes I presented them with a lure and would fire at them if they responded. Whereas I preferred to kill officers, the Russians were not fussy and would shoot at anybody. In our most advanced trench, more of our men were killed by snipers than by mortars and artillery. In some places there was no more than 200 metres between the respective front lines. Of course, if somebody on the other side raised his head into my line of fire he received a bullet.

The Russian snipers did the same. All it needed was too shallow a trench, giving them the opportunity to see movement in it, and a shot would crack out. This was the cause of three German deaths in the early hours of 3 July 1944.

I found my next five victims on the Slobodka–Chlobiczyn road on 4 July 1944. On the left flank of 7./Gren Regt 196, the Main Supply Route (*Rollbahn*), on an embankment, led into No Man's Land. To get their patrols out more safely, the Russians were excavating a deep narrow trench, which ran from their positions in the forest up to the shelter of the embankment. I was ordered to prevent this work proceeding. This required a lot of patience and a strong nerve. I settled down at spot height 376. At 0900 hrs a Russian raised his head above the trench. Although only visible for a couple of seconds, it was enough. I had him in the crosshairs and fired from 200 metres. He fell backwards (7).

On 10 October 1944 the official German Army High Command (Oberkommando des Heeres – OKH) newspaper, *Unser Heer* ('Our Army') carried an article entitled 'Alle Achtung vor Sutkus!', in which a comrade reported at length on several of my early missions. The first of these described the killing of victim number seven.

Left of the sector held by 7. Company of a grenadier regiment, the Bolsheviks were digging a running trench out to the raised *Rollbahn* in No Man's Land to create a protected departure point for their patrols. We could not stop them because they worked behind the embankment, and our own minefields deprived us of any element of surprise. It was therefore a task for our snipers. General excitement reigned in our trench. Could he do it? It would require a split-second assessment of the opportunity and then a lightning fast reaction.

There, just for a brief moment, we saw a pair of hands wielding a spade. Dear Ivan, now our sniper has seen you, just the least carelessness and you will pay the highest price for your activity!

Our sniper waits impassively behind his rifle. His features are drawn, nerves and muscles must not weaken. The East Prussian with his proverbial calm guarantees us that he will not miss when the moment comes. Time creeps by. Shovelfuls of earth continue to be tossed up, but the enemy soldier makes sure he exposes no part of his body. The shot cracks out! Just for a second the Ivan stretched and showed himself above the workings. It was enough. The shot through the head was fatal. The platoon commander observing from the trench thanks our sniper comrade with a handshake.

Half an hour later, from the company's left flank, I obtained a second shot from a range of 150 metres (*8*). In the evening I lay facing the entrenching operation 200 metres away. The Russians had put up a screen which made it very difficult for me to see anything, but the screen gave them a false sense of security and I got three more (*9*) (*10*) (*11*).

CLAIM NOS: *9, 10, 11*
DATE: *4.7.1944*
PLACE: *Slobodka-Lesna road, Sector 7./Gren Regt 196*
EVENT: *S. was instructed to take action against enemy digging a trench on the eastern side of the road facing 7. Company positions. Although his view was seriously obstructed by a screen which the enemy had put up to hide the activity, S. shot three Russian diggers in the head or chest. Range 200 metres Time: 2030–2200.*
WITNESSED: *Gefr Heplan*

I well remember those defensive battles in which the enemy attacked us and was repulsed. The Russians had the habit of leaving their dead and wounded where they fell in No Man's Land. We expected them to show at night with a retrieval detail, for we would never have left our own men lying there like that, but the Russians never came. A wounded Russian lay 150 metres from our trench and 120 metres from theirs. Naturally I did not shoot him. We thought they would send a party to bring him back when it fell dark. Next morning he was still there and writhing. We were outraged that the Russians would be so heartless as to allow one of their own to die like that.

My next five victims were surprised on 5 July 1944 along the Slobodka–Chlobiczyn road. I had taken up position in No-Man's Land fifty metres ahead of our minefield in 7. Company sector. As it grew light towards 0400 hours, I spotted a sniper on the enemy side. He was in a tree. I took him out with two rounds. He fell and ended up hanging from the branches (*12*). Earlier the Russians had pushed forward and set up a machine-gun nest, which I was able to make out. I got another sniper in my sights and we fired at each other simultaneously. I saw clearly how he collapsed just as his last bullet hit just in front of me (**13**). I also silenced the machine gun by taking out the three-man team at 200 metres (**14**) (**15**) (**16**).

CLAIM NOS: *12 to 16*

DATE: *5.7.1944*

PLACE: *Slobodka-Lesna road towards Chlobiczyn-Lesny, Sector 7./Gren Regt 196*

EVENT: *While engaging the Russian trench-diggers, S. became involved in a duel with a Russian sniper giving them cover, whom he shot from a tree with two rounds. Subsequently he silenced four Russians in advanced positions by occupying an exposed site fifty metres forward of our trench where he came under repeated enemy fire. Range 200 metres.*

WITNESS: *Lt Kaul*

A sniper has to bear many things in mind. His weapon must be calibrated exactly. I used to put out at a hundred metres distance a small label marked with a red spot smaller than my thumb. Then I made sure I could get a five-round group on the red spot. The sniper must be able to estimate distance accurately and gauge the wind speed and direction. Every detail is important. He relies on his abilities. He must never think he knows it all. In the Second World War the range always had to be estimated when on the march or in the trenches for there was no automatic-ranging facility available. Target seeking involved inspecting the terrain from top to bottom, left to right and back. I used to keep asking myself, am I looking at a natural feature here, or is it camouflage? Should those leaves be withering like that, the grasses drooping? The Russians were masters of camouflage. Their snipers were mostly from the taiga forests of Siberia and had grown up surrounded by nature.

Shooting had to be mastered and practised endlessly. The telescopic sight magnified the target four to six times for the sniper. Targets at 400 metres appeared to be at 100 metres. During aiming one can feel one's heartbeat. As soon as the target appeared at the centre of the crosshairs the trigger was squeezed. The pressure had to be very light so as not to disturb the line of the bullet's flight. It required a great deal of self-confidence to hit the target precisely. It is possible to be accurate up to 800 metres but success is more certain between 100 and 400 metres. There is no point in just shooting for shooting's sake. One has to hit the enemy, or he will hit you.

A company of our battalion had lost a number of men to enemy snipers, and I was called forward to look into the problem. My first act in the sector was to survey the terrain very precisely and decide where I would have chosen to be were I in the boots of our Soviet opponent. A sniper does not fire directly ahead but from an angle of about forty degrees in order to avoid rapid detection. One must have good cover and be well camouflaged in a position from where one has the best possible view of the enemy trenches. The range must be estimated as exactly as possible to ensure that the bullet does not fly too high or too low. Some snipers used tracer bullets. This was crazy, for it gave the enemy warning and enabled the source of fire to be pinpointed quicker.

The sniper had to avoid locating himself near an imposing feature – such as a large tree – which the enemy could recognise quickly to focus his search. The camouflage had to be chosen carefully to accord with nature. One must always think that the enemy sniper is one's equal, and always practise care and self-control, and remain confident. Nothing on one's clothing should present the enemy sniper with something to aim at. The most minor mistake would be enough to provide the enemy with a target. Upon sighting a target, one has to determine that it is a target and not a lure, then aim lightning fast – quicker than the opponent – to keep living.

I had fifty-two sniper duels and survived many of them only because the opponent misjudged the range and so fired too short or too high or failed to allow correctly for the wind. I am sure I had a sixth sense that enabled me to spot enemy snipers very rapidly. My weapon was a ZF-K98k (Zielfernrohr Karabiner 98 kurz) rifle with the low turret sight fitment and Zeiss Ajack 4x telescopic sight. Ammunition was important. I had special ammunition: the best was captured Yugoslavian and that of German pre-war manufacture, which gave tighter groups.

The sniper must always be aware of the position of the sun and take care that it never reflects from his field-glasses and so betrays his position. I had a special camouflage jacket issued only to snipers. It was earth-brown with a white lining and could be worn inside out if needed. It was hooded, of ample cut and was therefore comfortable in all shooting positions.

The rifle had to be cared for; the rifling needed to be perfectly clean and kept well oiled. One's life depended on this. The weapon had to be hung up and so stored so that it would not fall or be damaged. One always had to be able to rely on one's rifle. I was directly subordinate to the battalion commander. I was sent by him to a company for duty, and reported back to the battalion upon conclusion of a mission.

I found my next four victims in the Luna Schneise, or glade, north of Magyaren-Schlucht on 6 July 1944. I had gone out with two men from 5. Company. We had a reconnaissance mission to infiltrate woods occupied by the Russians, and to determine where they were working to build up and reinforce their trench system. While doing so we were spotted by a sentry. I had to shoot him (*17*). Soon afterwards I shot another as he was about to cross the glade (*18*).

CLAIM NOS: *17, 18*
DATE: *6.7.1944*
PLACE: *Luna Schneise near Magyaren-Schlucht, Sector 5./Gren Regt 196*
EVENT: *At 0500 S. with two witnesses worked forward in the woods opposite our position and put a Russian sentry out of action in the Luna Schneise with a shot to the head. A second Russian, attracted by the shot and crossing the Schneise was also shot down by S. Range: 300 metres.*
WITNESSES: *Uffz Herzel, Gefr Müller*

The *Unser Heer* article described this event in the following terms:

As dusk falls each evening the Soviets move up to the *Rollbahn*. About now they should appear again. Initially it is not possibly to determine in what strength they will occupy the sector. Their work recommences as they occupy one of their observation posts. Now and again, phantasma-like shadows flit in the confused tangle of underbrush, rather like wood spirits, more suggestion than flesh and blood. It needs excellent optics to bring these ghostly outlines into sharp focus. Only in combination with a very calm and sure hand will it be possible perhaps to shoot one of these shadowy forms. It is therefore a mission for our sniper again.

Carefully he observes the enemy's digging procedures. He imprints on his mind a picture of the target area, for after putting aside the binoculars he has to relocate the place in the featureless similarity of the forest edges. He embraces his rifle and takes the location in the sights. He has the target covered, but the form keeps vanishing. It is essential to retain the man in the optic triangle. How often he curls his finger round the trigger but does not squeeze it because all he now sees is the maze of branches in the crosshairs.

A trial of patience! Who has not heard stories of the angler's patience of an angel! A sniper's patience has been instilled with far more discipline. His prey does not take a hook or spinner.

His finger curls again. He fires! Over there the brown figure is distinguished against the pile of shovelled earth. A companion behind the dead or seriously wounded digger comes to render help, probing forward cautiously. After some hesitation he sets foot in the killing field. How can one blithely wander into a sniper's field of fire? Too late it occurs to him to take some cover behind the hill of earth. His shadow enters the aiming triangle of the sniper optic and after a resounding crack the second enemy soldier sinks to the cool floor of the forest.

Whilst advancing, a seven-strong scouting party detected us and manoeuvred to cut us off from the rear. I reacted at once, shot down the machine-gun carrier (**19**) and then pulled back to 5. Company positions. From there I shot a Russian in officer's clothing (**20**) near the timber barricade where the scouting party was moving. We returned to our unit without loss.

Claim Nos: *19, 20*
Date: *6.7.44*
Place: *Luna Schneise*
Event: *A quarter of an hour after shot No 18, S. noticed a seven-man enemy reconnaissance patrol approaching to his left at 150 metres distance. S. shot down the machine gunner No 1 and worked back to 5. Company position. From there he shot one Russian, apparently an officer, from the reconnaissance patrol in the area of the timber barricade. Range 150 metres*
Witnesses: *Uffz Herzel, Gefr Walther*

The *Unser Heer* article concluded with a description of this event:

Water drips from the leafy roof of the battalion's forest from where Gefreiter S. set out from 5. Company trenches at first light. Today he is making war on his own account. The discipline of the trenches and the wait for the enemy to show himself do not concern him today. He will seek out the enemy in his lair. After peering with great caution to both sides he pushes himself out over the trench. The group leader and another courageous man are his escorts. Their goal is the glade in enemy-held woodland beyond the Rollbahn. Metre by metre they slip through the narrow exit track, then the minefield and, ignoring the mud, snake over the supply road.

Now comes the daring part, the leap into the lion's den, into the woods. With a little misfortune they will fall into the arms of a Russian sentry. Such a mission as this requires a bit of good luck. They reach the glade. Gefreiter S. feels his way slowly along the edge of the wood and watches the pathways between the trees. There is a Soviet sentry between the trunks some distance away, but everything has been done so stealthily that the Russian notices nothing. Rifle up, calm aim, fire! Without a sound the sentry collapses between two trees. Our three watchers remain still as mice. Who knows how many eyes are now scouring the intervening space. A second Bolshevik arrives to attend his fallen colleague. He crosses the glade and the field of fire. A last step and he collapses. A good bag!

Cautiously, eyes watching for the enemy, the three retrace their steps along the edge of the glade. Suddenly to their left they detect a conversation in low tones. At 150 metres a seven-man scouting party comes into sight. Luckily, their blather has given them away! These chatterboxes present our courageous men with no danger. Sutkus aims at the machine gunner and shoots him in the head. The moment of confusion is used to retire to the German lines. The enemy scouting party is sufficiently imprudent to advance and peer into No-Man's Land from between the timber barricade. A gap in the barrier is enough for our experienced sniper. With calmness and certainty he searches out the distinctive clothing of the platoon leader who, to judge by the equipment being carried, must be an officer. A well-aimed shot to the head ends forever his peep into No Man's Land.

Thus our sniper has become an indispensable aid to his comrades in the forward trenches. Tenacious and determined during hours of long waiting, each of his well-aimed rounds spares his comrades much blood.

On 6 July 1944 I was awarded the Iron Cross 2. Class. The *Unser Heer* article described how I came directly from the trenches in my 'dirt-soiled camouflage wear' to receive the decoration from the hand of my Commanding Officer. After my twentieth success I received from my divisional commander a letter dated 7 July 1944: 'For your exemplary and outstanding achievements as a sniper, I express to you my very special recognition. Scheuerpflug, Generalmajor.'

On the morning of 7 July 1944 I was with 6. Company on the Slobodka–Chlobiczyn road. At 0330 hrs in the 'green hell' at the junction with 5. Company I hit a Russian sentry with a headshot from 200 metres (*21*). A quarter of an hour later I shot an infantryman who was firing on our positions with an SMG (sub machine gun) (*22*). I was now directed by 5. Company to the Luna Schneise north of Magyaren-Schlucht, where I climbed a tree to obtain a good view of the Russian positions. I saw movement, which I interpreted as the prelude to an attack. I identified a man as an officer by his uniform and deportment and shot him from 600 metres at 0700 hrs (*23*). We were able to repel the Russian attack and after that they left us in peace for a while, even calling off their artillery fire. I climbed another tree to observe the enemy positions and towards 2000 hrs saw a Russian crossing the glade. I shot him from 600 metres (*24*).

CLAIM No: *24*
DATE: *7.7.1944*
PLACE: *Luna Schneise*
EVENT: *In the evening S. was ordered to the Luna Schneise sector again to interrupt movement in the glade. At 600 metres range he shot down a Russian soldier attempting to cross it. Time: 2000 hrs*
WITNESS: *OberGren Behrend*

After this shot all hell broke loose and nine Russians who had spotted my perch began long periods of firing at me using MGs (machine guns) and SMGs. I stayed put in the tree and at 2015 hrs shot a machine gunner (*25*). Despite the enemy fire I edged to a screen from where at 200 metres I shot a Russian officer who was trying to reach cover (*26*).

CLAIM NOS: *25, 26*
DATE: *7.7.1944*
PLACE: *Luna Schneise*
EVENT: *About nine Russians who had identified S. as a sniper after shot No 24 opened fire on him with MGs and MPs (Machine Pistols, ie, sub machine guns). Nevertheless he remained in the tree and shot the machine gunner No 1 through the head. He shot a second gunner from a screen to which he had made his way under enemy fire. Range: 200 metres*
WITNESS: *OberGren Behrend Time: 2015 hrs*

On 9 July 1944 I obtained successes (**27**) and (**28**) in the Luna Schneise. We remained well camouflaged in No Man's Land and had to spend the night there. The enemy were scouring the ground ahead of their position in the search for us: we would have been discovered if we had moved. In the early hours of 10 July I hit an infantryman firing on our lines with an SMG (**29**). A second man with an SMG twenty metres away from him saw my hideout and fired at me. I hit him in the head from 180 metres at 0320 hrs (**30**).

On 11 July 1944 with 5. Company in the Magyaren-Schlucht I was attempting to ascertain the location of an enemy artillery spotter who appeared to have a good view of our trenches. This was no easy job because the enemy was in woods 800 metres away. A morning mist gave my observer and I cover to make our way forward. In No Man's Land within 280 metres of the enemy line we dug in, taking great care to perfect our camouflage. We were on a ridge with a good view over the surrounding countryside. As the mist cleared and the sun broke through I watched a Soviet artillery spotter climb a tree and settle on a platform in its branches, from where he examined our position through a scissors-periscope. I shot him with one round (**31**) and then destroyed his periscope with a second round when it glinted in the sunlight.

That evening I went to 2. Company/Gren Regt 188 at Slobodka-Lesna. The Russians were firing with artillery and mortars. I hit two gunners at 300 metres range (**32**) (**33**). An enemy assault troop about twenty strong combed No Man's Land for us. From our trenches grenadiers opened fire on the assault troop to enable my observer to crawl back to our lines using all available cover. Our battalion suffered losses.

On 11 July 1944 at Slobodka-Lesna I scored a third success (*34*). The following day I remained with 2. Company/Gren Regt 188. No Man's Land was between 800 and 1,000 metres wide at this point and not favourable for me. I worked myself forward 750 metres and from a rise had a good view over the enemy trench system. Following a thorough survey, I decided from the activity of their troops where the command bunker must be. At 1400 hrs an officer emerged from the bunker. I knew he was an officer by his cap – at the front other ranks wore steel helmets. I shot him (*35*) and another (*36*) who came out of the bunker to help. Range was 250 metres.

At the same location towards 0330 hrs on 13 July 1944 I shot a Russian soldier while in a tree 250 metres distant (*37*). After that I was recalled to the Magyaren-Schlucht and ordered to find and take out an enemy artillery spotter who was directing fire on our positions and causing us losses. I went forward of our front line and received fire from a Russian in a tree. From a ridge I managed to glimpse and shoot him (*38*). The search for the artillery spotter demanded a lot of patience. At 1800 hrs I finally recognised the well-camouflaged post in a tree and shot the spotter dead at a range of 300 metres (*39*).

Between 12 and 13 July 1944 I shot another five victims but these claims were not confirmed. Early on the morning of 14 July 1944 on the Slobodka-Lesna road I watched a Russian trying to put out a fire in a pile of brushwood. I shot him (*40*) and another Russian who was digging a trench (*41*).

On 17 July 1944 at Magyaren-Schlucht, I was positioned 250 metres forward of our front line and from a slight elevation could observe the terrain. At 300 metres I noticed two Russians in trees. I shot them both down (*42*) (*43*).

Claim Nos: *42, 43*
Date: *17.7.1944*
Place: *Magyaren-Schlucht, sector 5./Gren Regt 196*
Event: *S. worked forward about 250 metres ahead of the front line to an elevation from where he could better observe the terrain. From his hollow he shot two Russian forward observers in trees at a range of 300 metres.*
Witness: *OberGren Baumann*

At midday on 26 July 1944 I was on the Sloviska–Gisloviye road near spot height 234, running despatches from II Battalion to the Regimental Staff/Gren Regt 196, when I was surprised by a Russian assault platoon led by two officers who opened fire at me from 100 metres. I returned fire immediately and shot the two officers down (**44**) (**45**). I used the ensuing confusion amongst the enemy to change my position and from 200 metres shot two machine gunners (**46**) (**47**). The others then surrendered.

Claim Nos: *44 to 47*
Date: *26.7.1944*
Place: *Spot height 234*
Event: *Working as despatch runner for the battalion commander, S. came under infantry fire from about 100 metres from a Russian assault troop led by two officers. S. shot both, one after the other. Using the ensuing confusion amongst the Russians, S. changed his firing position and shot two machine gunners. Range: 200 metres*
Witness: *Lt [illegible]*

I sensed it on every occasion that I fell into the sights of an enemy sniper, and knew when he was just waiting for me to raise myself a little before shooting me. My instinct never betrayed me. Our unit was retreating from Lemberg in the Carpathians. We marched 120 kilometres in 24 hours, 100 kilometres the second day and 80 kilometres the third to take up positions in woodland where the water table was so high that we could not dig in – we struck water at one spade's depth. It was early autumn and raining. As we had not been issued greatcoats and had only our *gasplane* (protectice cape for gas attacks), we hung them from the branches of a fir to provide ourselves with some shelter from the rain. I was with the Battalion staff, which had some panzers. Naturally these practised no form of radio silence and after triangulating the bearings the enemy let us have a hurricane of artillery fire. Fortunately we had become accustomed to this. We could judge by the flight of the shells where they would land. Listening to their flight, you could tell when they would fly far and wide. You could hear them coming and then silence – then you were for it.

It was my turn to relieve the man on watch. I rose, people pulled me back. I was dead tired and allowed them to drag me down amongst them. 'Get up and relieve the sentry!' a voice ordered sternly. I forced myself to my feet, only to be pulled down again. Finally I tore free and went out to find the man on watch. Suddenly I seemed to be sucked up by the chest and hurled forward. A shell had landed amongst my comrades. The air pressure of the explosion catapulted me into a crater brimming with water. My friends lay torn and dismembered all around me. Shell splinters whirred overhead. I had survived miraculously once more.

I spent time at the fighting front with 5., 6. and 7. Companies. I had a precise knowledge of the terrain. One night at midnight I was summoned to the battalion CO, Hauptmann Hoffmann. He ordered me to proceed with one man to all three companies with orders that they should move to fresh positions unnoticed by the enemy. The landlines to the foremost trenches had been damaged by shelling, and so we had to locate each of these positions by following the damaged cabling. Hardly had we set out than my signals colleague was killed by a shell. I had to go on alone, with a mission on which many people's lives depended. The enemy had begun a fresh attack along all three sectors; bitter fighting had been raging for a week. Now and again the Russians had breached our lines but our counter-attacks usually managed to regain lost territory. The dead of both sides lay strewn everywhere.

In daylight the surroundings looked very different to how one saw them at night. It was dark, and trees I had down as markers lay toppled by the shelling. I felt that I had strayed off-course into No Man's Land. I stumbled over a body. I looked at his rucksack and cooking equipment attached, and smelt his sweat: this must be a Russian, I decided. When the dawn came I was horrified to see how close he was to our command bunker. He must have been going into it when he fell. I heard Russian voices! The enemy had captured it, and now some of them were emerging. It was too late to make my escape unseen. I dropped near the roadside, feigning death. Their boots crunched past me. Here is just another dead Fritz, they thought. Suddenly I jumped up and ran into the field of fire of 6. Company. Before they had a chance to react and shoot I shouted the password. They let me in and so I got through to 5. Company, where, by passing on the order to withdraw, I was able to save its complement of eighty men.

On 12 August 1944, at spot height 467, two kilometres east of Odrzechova, at 400 metres range I shot a Russian as he was rounding up horses (**48**).

CLAIM NO: *48*
DATE: *12.8.1944 Time 1700 hrs*
PLACE: *Spot height 467, two kms east of Odrzechova*
EVENT: *Whilst carrying out an order to round up loose horses left by the fleeing Russians, S. shot a Russian at 400 metres range with a shot to the chest.*
WITNESS: *Obergefr Buder*

In the early evening of the same day on a reconnaissance mission behind enemy lines in company with two men, on a road two kilometres east of Odrzecho a I saw a vehicle with a Soviet Major and several soldiers approaching. I shot one of the latter when he aimed a rifle at my comrade, Gefreiter Laschitsch (**49**).

CLAIM NO: *49*
DATE: *12.8.1944 Time 1815*
PLACE: *As No 48*
EVENT: *While carrying out a reconnaissance mission, S. shot a Russian with a shot to the chest in the instant when the latter was aiming at the observer. Range ten metres. From this mission the patrol brought in four soldiers and one Russian Major as prisoners.*
WITNESS: *Gefr Laschitsch*

We took the Major and four soldiers prisoner. I handed the major's attaché-case to the battalion staff. The attacks of 12 August 1944 on spot heights 467 and 474 north-west of Nadolany were noted in my diary as a confirmed close-combat day. (This was important for obtaining the award of the Infantry Assault badge (*Infanterie Sturmabzeichen*) in its various grades.) On 13 August I took part in the attack on a wood three kilometres north-east of Odrzechova, and then onwards through woodland rising to spot height 387.

From August 1944, our 68. Inf Div fought a rearguard action in the retreat from the Lemberg area. Our division was the last to leave the city, and headed into the Beskids.

On 4 September 1944, 1.3 kms north of Wroblik, at first light I was 100 metres ahead of our foremost lookout. Seeing several Russian forward observers pull back, I shot one at 300 metres (*50*). I shot another as he crawled away from his machine gun in order to identify my hideout (*51*). The witness was Uffz Wunderlich. Next day I moved out to the same position. Having reached my objective in the dark it was only a short time before I saw a light flare as a Russian lit a cigarette. I shot him from 300 metres (*52*). Again the witness was Uffz Wunderlich. Here I have to point out how stupid this was. The man thought nobody on the enemy side would see him smoking. But the sniper sees such things very well.

News of my successes had got around and my fifty-first confirmed claim was reported by 68. Inf Div to Corps and from there to Army. On 5 September 1944 I received from the Army Group Heinrici C-in-C, Generaloberst Heinrici, a telex with the following message: 'For his fifty-first success as sniper I express to Grenadier Sutkus my full recognition. I grant a special leave pass for fourteen days. Signed: Army Group C-in-C Heinrici.'

After my fifty-second success, on 19 September 1944, I received another letter in recognition, this time from the Commanding General, XXXXIX Gebirgskorps, General Karl von Le Suire: 'For his outstanding achievement as sniper, to Gefreiter Bruno Sutkus, 5./ Grenadier Regiment 196, my acknowledgement of his fifty-second success.'

On 5 December 1944, the front-line newspaper of 4. Panzer-Armee, *Raupe und Rad* ('Track and Wheel'), carried an article about me in two parts, drafted by Oberleutnant Schöppenthau, of which I reproduce the first part here. It was entitled: 'From Our Theatre of War – This is Sutkus!'

. . . We have the following interesting report on comrade Sutkus, who is attached to a grenadier regiment of our Panzer-Armee. 'He has been with us for about six months. At first we knew absolutely nothing about him. Of course, he was a fine chap, a good comrade like any other, but there was nothing particular about him which caught your eye. A few days after he arrived with the last batch of replacements and our battalion adjutant had exchanged some welcoming words with him, in response to my enquiry he told me,

"Jawoll, Herr Leutnant, tough as the panzers!" That was nothing special, East Prussians are supposed to be like that.

'It was not until he was put at the battalion's hottest spots and within a short time had claimed ten – twenty – thirty – yes forty and even fifty victims that we took notice of him. Good heavens, that was extraordinary. It was something we had never expected of this happy-go-lucky but otherwise modest and unassuming East Prussian forest worker. Naturally, recognition was not long in coming. His general, who had marked his thirtieth victim with a special allocation of chocolate and from then on took a keen interest in his successes, rewarded him after his fiftieth confirmed claim with the Iron Cross 2. Class.'

I spent my fourteen days' special leave with my parents. I found them at Blumental, to where they had been evacuated. The front was edging ever nearer the German border. Would the Russians soon occupy German territory? I thought often of my parents and sister. How would they fare when the Russians arrived? This was an incentive to keep me fighting. The German people had already made so many sacrifices – was it all to have been in vain? On 7 September I was awarded the Wound badge in black.

# 4

## *A Grim Vision of What to Expect: My Tally Rises to 130 Victims*

The desperate defensive battle for the Carpathian mountain passes began on 8 September 1944. Generaloberst Heinrici had taken overall command of 1. Panzer-Armee and 1st Hungarian Army to form Armee-Gruppe Heinrici, which then joined Heeresgruppe A on its right flank. Our 68. Inf Div was involved in the main fighting south of Sanok-Krosno. Numerous Russian tanks were destroyed by courageous grenadiers in fighting at close quarters. On 16 September 1944, 68. Infantry Division received a Mention in the *Wehrmacht Report*.

The Russian intention was to break through Heinrici's north flank in the Beskids and wheel south to attack the south-facing front of Heeresgruppe Süd on the Hungarian plain. Along the length of the Eastern Front the Soviets were being resisted in the most bitter fighting.

On 16 October 1944 a rumour spread through our lines like wildfire: the Russians were in East Prussia! They had set foot on German soil south of Gumbinnen. For us this was unimaginable. All available German forces were being thrown against the Soviets. The fighting in East Prussia was conducted by the Red Army with methods of unparalleled barbarity. Nobody – soldier or civilian – was safe on German soil in the presence of a Russian soldier. The lower ranks had been stirred up by their superiors: in an Order of the Day, General Ivan Chernyachovski ordered his men: 'There must be no mercy, the Fascists' land must be made into a desert!'

The East Prussian village of Nemmersdorf was recaptured by German forces. German women, men and children had been murdered there by the Russians. Women had been crucified on barn doors after being gang-raped. Men, women, even babes in arms were bludgeoned to death, shot or drowned. Even French forced labourers were not spared. Germany's eastern peoples experienced an inferno, totally defenceless against the vile brute that was the Russian soldier. These were not atrocities committed by lone sadists or small units, but in pursuance of clearly verifiable instructions issued by Soviet political and military leaders to the units. Even the Russian Army Staffs received orders before they reached German territory that could only be interpreted as an incitement to murder and pillage. On 5 January 1945 Soviet Marshal Zhukov issued an order to 1st White Russian Front (Army Group): 'The time has come for the reckoning with the German Fascist blackguards. We have a huge burning hate . . . this time we will destroy the German vermin once and for all.'

For years, with primitive tirades of hate, the writer Ilya Ehrenburg had been urging Soviet soldiers to consider the Germans as wild beasts and kill them as such. The war had thus entered its final phase. Now each of us was aware, knowing the unspeakable atrocities of which the Red Army was capable, what we were fighting for. Our duty was to protect our families and our eastern provinces against the Soviets.

After my leave I returned to II Battalion/Gren Regt 196. Many familiar faces were missing. Our companies were facing the enemy at Kruzlova. The Russans had broken through our main front line and encircled us. Then they began to tighten the noose. We had set up a new defensive line two kilometres north-north-east of Kruzlova, and on 25 October 1944 I shot two Russian officers at 150 metres range (*54*) (*55*). During an attack on the battalion command post, Oberfeldwebel Kestler of 8. Company pointed out a heavy machine gun firing on our men. I shot two men serving this weapon (*56*) (*57*). A Russian officer then appointed two men to replace the dead gunners, and I shot these replacements from eighty metres (*58*) (*59*) and also the officer (*60*) as he tried to get to cover. During our counter-attack I saw a Russian officer desert his men and run, and I shot him down (*61*). Our counter-attacks regained our battalion command post, and the Russians decided to retreat from our lines altogether. During this manoeuvre I shot two more (*62*) (*63*). Our wounded, whom we had been forced to leave when the Russians crossed our lines, were found murdered, two with a bullet to the neck, the other by small-arms fire.

On 27 October 1944, two kilometres north-north-east of Kruslova, while at the front in 5./Gren Regt 196 sector, during heavy fire from infantry and artillery on our positions, I saw several Russians break cover and storm our trenches, driven forward by an officer with pistol drawn. I shot the officer first (*64*) and then from forty metres a Russian soldier who was making his way towards us with belligerent intent from a machine-gun nest (*65*).

Finally we had an influx of new men. Our battalion received a second sniper. It was autumn, it rained and snowed, it was cold and we were soaked through, and we had still not received our winter clothing. We went a whole week without food and lived in our trenches. Several times the Soviets captured our infantry trenches after fierce fighting. We received reinforcements, counterattacked and ejected the enemy. All this caused us great losses, but we succeeded in holding the line.

The new sniper received an order to engage enemy snipers. He found himself a position. His first shot missed, and it was his last because the enemy sniper shot him in the head. This was a major lesson for me as well: not only my own life, but also the lives of the company to which I had been detached that day depended on my continuing accuracy. Snipers helped out in the most forward sectors of the front and protected the infantry against enemy snipers. For this reason they were feared and hated by the enemy. Accuracy guaranteed my life. A second newly arrived sniper was seriously wounded a short while later and was invalided out. Thus I remained the battalion's only sniper.

On 29 October 1944 in the same location as the two previous successes, after a short period of observation I took out a Russian machine gunner who had a 5./Gren Regt 196 machine-gun nest under well-aimed fire (*66*). While behind a tree during an artillery bombardment, I took out three Soviets at forty metres who had broken cover to fire on our position with infantry weapons (*67*) (*68*) (*69*). Feldwebel Durawa of 6./Gren Regt 196 indicated some well-camouflaged Russians firing on our positions. After a brief survey I saw them and shot two consecutively (*70*) (*71*). Next, Feldwebel Durawa accompanied me to 6. Company positions and indicated sources from where infantry fire frequently hit our men and caused losses. Here I discovered three well-camouflaged Soviets – a sniper, an officer and an observer. It appeared that they were directing the artillery and mortar fire. I got the sniper first (**72**). The officer tried to run for it and I shot him down (**73**) and then the observer at a range of forty metres as well (**74**). Witnesses were Feldwebel Durawa, Obergefreiter Wagner, Gefreiters Bitta, Lasch and Kneppert. My battalion CO, Major Herbert Hoffmann, was decorated with the German Cross in Gold on 29 October 1944.

On 30 October 1944 two kilometres north-north-east of Kruzlova the Russians were edging closer to our front line in the prelude to an attack. Ahead of our trenches a quick-response unit had been installed, and I joined their number. We came under well-aimed fire. At that I crept fifty metres forward of our lines and shot two Russian forward observers from a range of twenty metres (**75**) (**76**). The witness was Gefreiter Bitta.

It was damp and cold. It seemed to have been raining nonstop for ages. We had to scoop out water from our trench, our boots were soggy; we were unable to remove clothing to dry it. Many of our men were sick and our positions were manned by one man every hundred metres in some places. At night one man could not see the next and never knew if he were still alive when the enemy subjected our lines to attack.

I had been bailing water from the trench to get the level below that of the plank we stood on. I saw my comrade Horst raise himself a little to peer over the parapet. The enemy spotted him and he was hit by an MG round. As he collapsed I caught him to prevent his fall into the trench waters. He was bleeding from the back. I was about to apply a dressing but he waved it away, knowing that he was done for. I asked if he were in great pain; he said it felt like he had been pierced by hot needles. Then in a weak voice he begged me to write to his mother with news of his death at the front so that she and his wife should not wait for his return. With glazed eyes he called for his mother and died.

In 6. Company sector, two kilometres north-east of Kruzlova, at first light on 31 October 1944 I proceeded with Gefreiter Steffes as observer beyond our front line into No Man's Land – to an elevation from where I could see the Russian positions in front of the village of Pisana and the nearby military highway. A lot of regulated traffic flowed along this thoroughfare. We dug in and camouflaged. When the mist lifted we had a wonderful view of the village. Some enemy tanks were standing ready to attack, and a large Russian convoy passed by. I identified two senior Russian officers and shot them both from 500 metres (*77*) (*78*). Immediately an awesome infantry, mortar and artillery response began. As our hiding place was forty degrees off centre we were not in danger. It was time to move on, however, since the protective mist was now dispersing. On the way back to our lines we were detected by a Soviet MG nest at Pisana, which fired at us. From 500 metres I picked off the gunner (*79*).

In 5. Company sector on 2 November 1944 the Russians had crept up very close to our trenches. Feldwebel Mirr gave me a report and showed me roughly from where the enemy was observing us and firing. After long observation I made out a well-camouflaged MG nest and shot the Soviet gunner through the head (*80*). I then made my way to 6. Company sector where Unteroffizier Baldauf pointed out a place that was receiving frequent fire from a concealed Russian wielding an SMG. After a while the Russian decided to return to his lines and I shot him from fifty metres (*81*). After we sustained further losses from a Russian MG nest I shot two more from fifty metres (*82*) (*83*).

On 3 November 1944 in 5. Company sector I snaked out fifteen metres ahead of our lines. A Russian spotted me, but seemed to think I was one of them, possibly because of my brown camouflage jacket. I shot him from twenty metres (*84*). At the same moment an enemy sniper fired at me. His bullet ricocheted off my steel helmet and inflicted a wound over my left eye, which bled. His observer changed position and I shot him (*85*). A pair serving an MG sighted me and opened fire from fifty metres: I took them both out (*86*) (*87*).

At this time the fighting was very fluid and we were subjected to sporadic heavy artillery fire. Thus we ate irregularly. A runner came by, bringing us ammunition and reporting that provisions had arrived behind our line in a ruined village. The Feldwebel appointed two men to fetch the food. In each hand they carried four mess tins, and eight water bottles on a strap around their necks. Besides these they had a sack for bread, butter, sausages and ammunition. The enemy was no more than 300 metres distant –

they had noticed the movement and heard the clatter of mess tins. The Russians then began to rake our positions with MG fire and bombard us with artillery. When the food messengers had not returned within a reasonable period of time I was sent out to locate them. They were fifty metres from our lines, both shot through the chest by an MG burst. To the end they must have been still thinking of their hungry comrades, for the mess tins had been put down neatly on the level to ensure that none of the precious contents were spilled. With tears in my eyes I carried the food into the trenches.

We moved to Jastrzebiec. At first light on 15 November 1944 in 7. Company sector I watched a Russian sniper firing on our positions. I shot him through the chest from 400 metres (*88*). There was a command post in the same sector. At 0730 hrs I shot a Russian officer from 500 metres as he left a bunker in the company of other officers (*89*). Next I shot three more officers in the group from the same range (*90*) (*91*) (*92*). One of their snipers had been following this – 7. Company had been aware of him for some time as being responsible for quite a few losses on our side. Now he knew my position and shot at me. I confirmed his position by seducing him into firing at a lure, and then finished his career with a shot to the chest from 500 metres (*93*).

From the same lair I noticed Russian soldiers planting some fir trees along the roadside. This was done to block our view. After our artillery flattened some of these trees I had the road in plain sight again. Soon a horse and carriage came along, a coachman in charge. The carriage had several occupants. I shot the horse, which brought the carriage to a stop in an excellent position to finish off the occupants. I hit one man seated (*94*) and a second as he attempted to alight (*95*). The coachman leapt down and got a round off but it was well wide of me, as I had moved forty degrees to one side to avoid being a target. When the coachman remounted the carriage I shot him from 500 metres (*96*).

That night a patrol returned with a prisoner who stated under interrogation that a German sniper had shot a general, a commissar, a regimental commander and a battalion commander in front of a bunker. These were my victims (*89*) to (*92*) above. In Soviet captivity, long after the war, I was interrogated by Colonel-General Miroshnitshenko at Irkutsk regarding these shootings and learnt the circumstances. The senior officers were members of an inspectorate that had the task of investigating an attack by the Russian air force on our positions a few days before. Their ground forces had had a secret command base, which decided to fire starshells over our positions to show their bombers where to drop their loads, but the bombers dropped on the secret command base instead, thus identifying it for us and enabling us to capture it without difficulty. The inspectorate had arrived to find the officer responsible for the disaster. The members of the investigating party had been warned as to the presence of a dangerous German sniper in that particular sector of the front. They chortled. They were certainly not going to be intimidated by a single German rifleman; the inability of the local Russian forces to eliminate him only served to show their incompetence.

We knew the inspectorate would be coming. One of our night patrols had lifted a prisoner from their trenches and he told all he knew. They would be coming next morning. I was given my orders. The inspectorate had to pass our way and we had a good view of the bend. It was swampy there and only one path existed. Colonel-General Miroshnitshenko had been a commissar in that same sector of the front at the time. He said that my name was well known to them. This was obvious to me, for their loudspeaker addresses often referred to me by name as 'the bloodiest Fascist' and always signed off with the most lurid threats to annihilate me. All their efforts at entrapment – their snipers laid in wait in countless ambushes – failed. Gradually they were becoming paranoid at the way I kept picking off their men one after the other, and now nobody on their side felt safe any more. The slightest wrong move in the trenches and someone received a bullet to the head. Thus I cleansed the sector of many enemy snipers and so spared our grenadiers.

In the same area that day I saw a Russian running towards a farmyard opposite 7. Company sector and shot him in the chest from 700 metres (**97**). With Lt Jensen I also noticed a Russian bailing water from a trench. When he showed himself above the parapet I shot him (**98**). Whilst proceeding from 7. Company command post to II Battalion with Lt Jensen, Unteroffizier Schäfer, Obergefreiter Adler and Gefreiter Koller, a Russian sniper fired two rounds at Lt Jensen and myself. It took me some time to locate the sniper's position, but when he changed his hiding place, I shot him from 450 metres (**99**).

At dawn on 16 November 1944 at Jastrzebiec I watched a platoon of Russian soldiers move out of their trench and advance towards the farmyard. I identified the officer leading them and shot him from 400 metres (**100**). I also shot two men dragging a heavy machine gun (**101**) (**102**).

The circumstances surrounding my hundredth victim were described by Oberleutnant Schöppenthau in the 4. Panzer-Armee newspaper *Raupe und Rad*, in the 5 December 1944 edition:

> The story of Sutkus's 100th to 102nd successes deserves a special mention. It came about like this. Sutkus had shot his 99th Ivan, a Soviet sniper who had fired on him while proceeding from battalion to company, forcing him to take cover. Sutkus shot him almost in passing as his opponent attempted to change position shortly afterwards. By error this claim was reported to battalion and regiment as number one hundred, the regiment naturally emphasising the event with the observation: 'You can see we have some sniper here!'
>
> Shortly afterwards his personal file was requested for the award of the Iron Cross 1. Class. This gave rise to a difficulty – the error had meanwhile come to light – it was not number one hundred! The battalion was urged to ensure that Sutkus shot another Ivan by next morning. How he should do this the regiment was not prepared to say. We went to bed with mixed feelings. Next morning a cautious telephone enquiry: 'Has S. perhaps . . . ?' A moment's silence at the other end. Tense expectation and impatience on the part of the caller, then the battalion CO drawled: 'Yes, do you know, dear boy, we sent Sutkus out and he has just submitted his 102nd confirmed claim!'

In 7. Company sector on 16 November 1944 I saw two Russians take up position in a ruin. As they moved out towards one of their company command posts that we knew of, I shot one (**103**), the other stood transfixed with shock and made himself an easy target (**104**); range was 400 metres. Also in 7. Company sector I saw Russians bailing water out of their bunker. From 400 metres I shot three (**105**) (**106**) (**107**) as they crawled out. After that I saw a Russian bunny-hopping along a trench towards a bunker. He was wearing a cap, and since other ranks wore steel helmets in the trenches, I identified him as an officer. As he prepared to make another hop I shot him from 350 metres (**108**).

---

Closely surveying the territory before us, I noticed the quantity of troops the Russians had in their front line. We never had a third of that number. At 600 metres I saw a Russian laden with mortar bombs making his way forward and shot him (**109**). My witnesses were Obergrenadier Jarosch, Grenadiers Roeder and Peter Haas, and Gefreiters Lennek and Hülsemann.

On 16 November 1944, following my hundredth success, I received as a private soldier of Grenadier Regiment 196/68. Infantry Division the award of the Iron Cross 1. Class.

On 19 November 1944 during a mission in 5. Company sector near Przyboro I was recognised by an enemy MG nest. I saw their muzzle flash and went to ground at once. The burst whistled overhead from 500 metres; one round struck a stone and rebounded, hitting me above the right eye. When the machine gunner attempted to leave his position I shot him from 500 metres (**110**). A sniper who had progressed towards our lines must have seen me shoot victim 110 and fired at me. The bullet came at an angle, ricocheted and tore a patch from the cover of my steel helmet. Once again I had been very lucky. This sniper had presumably been sent out specifically to hunt me. This was the same sector in which I had shot the inspectorate officers on 15 November. As soon as the sniper had inched to one side I had him lightning fast in the crosshairs and hit him in the head from 300 metres (**111**). The witness was Obergrenadier Balz. My forehead wound was treated and covered with a plaster, after which I returned to duty.

In the field only the strong and lucky man survives. I saw how comrades who dozed near me were torn apart by artillery. Others were shot down in the trenches. A young soldier broke under the strain and deserted to the rear. He was detained and handed over to the field police, court-martialled in the field and sentenced to death. We all had to witness the execution.

The Russians did not appear to have anything resembling military law. In July 1942, when their armies were in flight and panic reigned, whoever failed to obey the order to stand and fight was shot on the spot on Stalin's order. When their troops stormed our trenches, they needed commissars and other 'specialists' behind their men to drive them forward, and whoever did not want to go forward was shot in the back. Casualty figures were irrelevant to them.

On one occasion we were unable to contain an attack on our lines. Reinforcements came up and sealed the breach. Our eleven comrades that we had not been able to take with us as we retreated were found murdered – either by a shot to the back of the head or bayonetted.

Soviet snipers had no compunction about shooting our soldiers wherever the chance presented itself. That is the way of warfare. I received the order to spot these snipers and kill them. According to the Russians this was a war crime. I was actually an auxiliary in the foremost trenches saving our grenadiers' lives. I risked my life for them. The enemy was equally ruthless, but I had more luck than they did, even though they often had me in their sights.

In a duel between snipers the survivor was the one with the better technique. This required practice day and night, and self-mastery. I was certain of my marksmanship, as well as my knowledge of terrain, from my childhood spent along the Scheschuppe River between the German Reich and Lithuania. I used to pick out the border guards and work out how to smuggle contraband past them without being seen. Controlling my panic when sneaking between Lithuanian and German customs officials resulted in no small way from my knowing the territory and adopting a very good camouflage. As a boy I would enter the farmer's orchard furtively to steal his apples. I had to keep a good lookout for the gardener, who would inform my father if he saw me there, which meant a beating.

My father fell ill and from the age of sixteen I filled his shoes as a farm worker on the Fichtenhöhe estate. I had to plough using a team of four horses; at harvest time, and when threshing the corn in early autumn I had to carry 300 sacks up to the second floor of the barn. It was hard and difficult work. Nevertheless it was a foundation for what I was to encounter at the front, while 'Mummy's boys' who had been pampered had a mountain to climb. Thus my early life on the German–Lithuanian frontier was a kind of pre-military training.

I grew up with nature and recognised its changes. When Russian snipers hoisted a lure I was never deceived: I knew their intentions and their location. A sniper must know nature in every detail. Then he will see what is natural and what is camouflage. The inability to recognise the smallest change will curtail one's life at the front. A sniper must be confident of his abilities and shoot very precisely. This requires endless practice and instils calm and freedom from tension. Nervousness transmits itself to the telescopic sight. And I have never smoked, not even at the front.

On 21 November 1944 I was awarded the Sniper Proficiency Badge Grade 3. By then I had long exceeded the qualifying mark of sixty confirmed claims. I received the preliminary certificate for this highest of all distinctions for a German sniper, but the award itself – the cloth sniper badge – I never received.

The Führer-Order (*Führerbefehl*) instituting the Sniper Proficiency Badge (*Scharfschützenabzeichen*) was published in the gazette *Allgemeine Heeresmitteilungen* of 7 September and 7 October 1944.

Führer-Order 34. Order of the Führer for the introduction of the Sniper Proficiency Badge.

Der Führer                                     Higher Führer HQ, 20.8.1944

1. In recognition of the importance of the role of the lone rifleman as a marksman and to applaud the successes achieved to date, I introduce the Sniper Proficiency Badge for the Army and Waffen-SS. The Sniper proficency badge will be awarded in three grades.
2. Implementation regulations will be laid down by the General of Infantry to the Chief of the Army General Staff.
   Signed, Adolf Hitler.

Implementation regulations applying to the Führer-Order of 20 August 1944 regarding the introduction of the Sniper Proficiency Badge.

The Führer has introduced a Sniper Proficiency Badge for the Army and Waffen-SS. Its purpose is to highlight the importance of the rifle marksman and laud his successes with single aimed shots while providing at the same time an incentive to increase the tally of successes achieved to date. Accordingly the Sniper Proficiency Badge will be awarded on the following basis:

1. The Sniper Proficiency Badge will be awarded by the next highest front-line senior officer with at least the authority of a

regimental commander, on the written recommendation of the unit commander, to those soldiers who have received scheduled sniper training and have been employed as such. The person receiving the award is to be notified by certificate and the award is to be noted in his personal identification papers. (See Annexe 2) [*not reproduced here*].

2. The proficiency badge (see Annexe 1) [*not reproduced here*] is separated into three grades and will be worn on the right forearm. Where a soldier wears a badge denoting a specialist function and grade, or is awarded one together with the Sniper Proficiency Badge, the former is to be worn below the Sniper Proficiency Badge.

3. The awards are: Grade 1 for at least twenty shot enemy as from 1.9.1944 (badge without special edging), Grade 2 for at least forty shot enemy as from 1.9.1944 (badge with silver cord edging) and Grade 3 for at least sixty shot enemy as from 1.9.1944 (badge with gold-yellow cord edging). Claimed successes during close combat will not be counted. Moreover the enemy must have been shot while still capable of movement and not have been showing the intention to cross to our lines or to surrender.

4. Every claimed success requires a report to be made to the unit and confirmation by at least one witness. Units will draw up Sniper lists to conform with annexed Schedule 3 based on reports submitted. An extract from the Sniper list is to be supplied on transfer to a new unit together with other necessary documents. In order to avoid unnecessary correspondence a retrospective submission of claimed successes is not required. It is suggested as much more suitable that previous achievements should honoured when awarding the Iron Cross.

Oberkommando des Heeres, 20.8.1944
General of Infantry to the Chief of the Army General Staff

# 5

## *Jastrzebiec, My Last Battlefield: Ninety-Eight More Victims*

In the autumn at Jastrzebiec it rained frequently with snowfall. The trenches filled with water. In summer one could undress, dry one's clothing and pick out lice. Now we trembled with cold, wrapped ourselves in our *gasplane* and warmed each other. Making a fire was naturally out of the question since the enemy would have seen it at once and reacted.

On 22 November 1944 I was in 7. Company sector and saw two Russians bailing water from their trench 450 metres away. I shot one (*112*) and another who came on the scene to render him aid (*113*). At first light I made out an enemy MG position which had advanced to within 250 metres of our lines and was well camouflaged. I shot the gunner through the head (*114*). I spotted the gleam of the sun on an optic and had the sensation that I was in somebody's sights. Suddenly a shot rapped out that narrowly missed my neck. It was the Russian sniper's last shot, for I soon had him in the crosshairs and squeezed the trigger (*115*). That same moment a second sniper fired at me, but his aim was a little too high, and the bullet glanced off my steel helmet. Both these snipers had concealed themselves behind a wall. I shot the second in the chest from 200 metres (*116*). Thus I had shot two enemy snipers the same morning, a rare occurrence. The witness was Obergrenadier Berres.

Next day I was with 7. Company again. I saw two Russians running, probably carrying despatches, and shot one at 400 metres (*117*). The other took cover but after what he thought was a suitable length of time decided to crawl away, resulting in his becoming a victim (*118*). I saw a sentry, and after keeping him under observation for a long period shot him when he was relieved from his post and wandered away without due heed (*119*). The range was 300 metres, and witnesses were Gefreiter Lichtenburger and Grenadier Buttner. [*The following victims appear in the author's sniper log with incorrect dates and are re-arranged correctly here.*]

At first light on 21 November 1944 I placed myself in a position giving me an improved view and I noticed how the Russians had become much more cautious. Nevertheless I spotted a sentry who had been relieved and was returning to his bunker, and I shot him from 400 metres (*120*). An infantryman with an SMG replied and after concentrated observation I hit him from the same range (*121*); my witness was Gefreiter Lichtenberger. On 22 November 1944 I observed Soviet soldiers building a bunker. I shot two of them from 400 metres (*122*) (*123*). I also saw some Russians retiring from their advanced night trench to the day trench and shot two (*124*) (*125*) from about 300 metres. This was witnessed by Gefreiters Brodnack and Madus.

The following day, 23 November, I received from the C-in-C, 4. Panzer-Armee, General der Panzertruppe Fritz-Hubert Gräser, a letter in acknowledgement of my seventy-fifth success. This had been achieved some time previously, for my tally to date was by then 125.

In celebration of my 111th success, on 20 November 1944 I had received a letter in acknowledgement from the Commanding General, XXXXVIII Panzer-Korps, Generalleutnant Maximilian Reichsfreiherr von Edelsheim. He also sent me a parcel full of valuable goods. On 25 November 1944 the *Wehrmacht Report* stated: 'Sniper Grefreiter Sutkus of Grenadier Regiment 196 has claimed 125 enemy victims within five months.'

On 28 November 1944 in 7. Company sector near Jastrzebiec I observed lively movement on the supply road. The Russians would have felt secure under the cover of a light mist. I was 300 metres ahead of our lines and had a good view of the enemy. I shot a well-dressed Russian through the chest at 400 metres (*126*). I shot down a second when he suddenly stopped moving (*127*). The witness was Grenadier Elmer. In the same location on the same day, while observing the terrain, I was detected by a Russian sniper. Under my camouflage jacket I was wearing a thickly-layered protective waistcoat that was relatively bullet-proof at 400 metres – I decided to risk receiving a shot to the chest. His bullet hit me there fair and square. I feigned dead and kept my sights on the enemy sniper. Once he eventually left his hiding place, I shot him from behind (**128**). This was witnessed by Grenadier Elmer. Later that day our mortars and artillery pounded a property behind the Russian positions. After the bombardment finished, I saw many Russian soldiers running about. Two of these appeared to be trying to restore order. I shot them both at 350 metres (**129**) (**130**). The witness was Gefreiter Lichtenberger.

Our regimental CO at this time was Major Schulze. After my unbroken service at the front on the bend of the Vistula, on 24 November 1944 I was given leave from the front and spent a week in the Soldiers' Convalescent Home (*Soldatenheim*), a former sanatorium, at Busko, not far from the lines. When I arrived there, the duty German Red Cross nurse, Erika Lenz, sat me next to her at a table. She watched with interest my careful operations to clean my sniper rifle and my boots. Without speaking, she took my camouflage jacket, holed by several Russian bullets, and began to sew the tears. 'Go to the cinema,' she told me. When I returned I found my jacket nicely repaired. On another occasion she gave me her pudding as a second helping. Erika was a very attractive girl and I liked her. I began to think about her day and night. I found myself singing the well-known soldiers' song of the time, 'Erika':

> *Auf der Heide blüht ein kleines Blümelein.*
> *Und das heisst, Erika.*

(On the heath there blooms a tiny little flower.
And its name is Erika).

I locked this tiny little flower deep in my heart. She seemed to like me too, for she always paid me special attention. Yet I knew she was beyond my reach. I was a simple soldier and could fall victim at any moment in a sniper duel with the enemy. I never thought for a moment that I should spend all my Wehrmacht service in the most advanced position and still emerge alive at the end of it.

My period of rest and recuperation lasted until 8 December 1944, when I returned to the battalion. I went forward again at

Jastrzebiec. At first light on 9 December I was with 5. Company. I watched a Russian sentry being relieved at the farmstead and then shot him, range 300 metres (*131*).

I observed another Russian who was walking back and forth to keep warm and left cover. I shot him in the chest from 300 metres (*132*). Another Russian turned up, probably to relieve the second one: I shot him (*133*). From 400 metres range I also shot a soldier proceeding from their trenches to the farmstead (*134*). Next a Russian emerged from a bunker and started bailing water – I shot him in the chest (*135*). Another one who came to see what his comrade was doing I shot in the chest from 300 metres (*136*). The Soviet machine gunners must have finally noticed all this because my position now came under fire. Their bullets whistled close by over my head. I crawled away successfully to another position, for the Russians did not see me move and continued to fire on my previous position. I now had a better view of them and kept surveillance on the two machine gunners from 300 metres until I shot them both (*137*) (*138*).

Later in the day I watched the change of sentries 300 metres away. I shot one sentry in the chest and saw him collapse (*139*). This led to two more arriving to lend a hand, range between 300 and 320 metres (*140*) (*141*). Witnesses were Obergefreiter Erich Schmidt, Grenadier Richard Novak, Gefreiters Max Bartel, Matschik and Anton Dubail, all from 5. Company/Gren Regt 196.

~

*68. Infantry Division could do nothing about the 25 square kilometre Russian bridgehead over the Vistula River. The Russians outnumbered the Germans in infantry eleven to one and in tanks twenty-five to one, yet achieved very poor territorial gains in local fighting in their attempts to break out. The enemy was assembling ever more troop concentrations in the Baranov bridgehead. This indicated a major offensive, presumably scheduled for January 1945 when all swamps and rivers would be frozen over and their spearhead units would encounter no further geographical obstructions.*

~

At 2300 hrs on 9 December 1944 the Russians began their attack. Heavy artillery rained down fire on our front line. We could beat off an attack of regimental size but not this. Gren Regt 196 received the order to move out. Major Hoffmann, the battalion CO, gave me orders for delivery to the most advanced units because the telephone connections had been severed and I knew the way. I had done this kind of thing a few months before. I was accompanied by a colleague from the signals platoon who was to repair the damage to the telephone lines. The orders stated that the forward companies were to disengage at 0300 hrs, if possible without the enemy noticing the withdrawal. These companies were actually little more than remnants, for all of them had suffered heavy losses in the past two weeks of fighting and had been reduced to less than half their authorised strength.

We had just arrived forward when my companion was killed by a mortar round. Now I had to deliver the orders alone. It was no simple matter to find the units, for the terrain looked different by night. The Russian artillery fire forced me to take cover frequently. Eventually I managed to get the withdrawal order to all units before the deadline. We carried our wounded with us. Our company commander, Oberfeldwebel Roller, was seriously wounded in one lung by a shell splinter. I helped carry his stretcher and we got him to the dressing station, but he died there an hour later of internal bleeding. During their various attacks the Russians suffered very heavy losses.

On 10 December 1944, with 8. Company near Jastrzebiec, I was shown a well-camouflaged Russian MG nest. After several hours' observation I watched this gun fire on our front line. I shot a Russian in the chest from 350 metres as he left the position (*142*), the witness was Gefreiter Trepka.

On 11 December 1944 with 7. Company, accompanied by Unteroffizier Kühn as observer, I shot a Russian sentry on watch from 450 metres (*143*). From the same position I saw a Russian soldier leave a house and proceed from there in an easterly direction. I shot him from 500 metres (*144*). Later I saw some Soviets entering and leaving a bunker near the Jastrzebiec demesne, and succeeded in shooting an officer through the chest at 400 metres (*145*). Witnesses were Uffz Kühn and Gefreiter Odenthal, 7./Gren Regt 196.

On 16 December, near Kargov, I observed a Russian sentry post on the Karnickelberg and shot the sentry from 250 metres (*146*), and another in the chest who came running up to render assistance (*147*). Next day I shot another sentry on the Karnickelberg from 250 metres at the change of sentries (*148*) and a second man proceeding from the Karnickelberg into the woods (*149*). Subsequently I saw a Russian sniper go to cover with an observer. First I shot the observer through the head from 250 metres (*150*), observed by Gefreiter Dubail: the victim was careless and showed himself while viewing our positions through binoculars. There now followed the duel with the sniper. We fired simultaneously: I hit him in the head (*151*), his bullet missed me. Dubail witnessed this exchange.

CONFIRMED CLAIMS: *150/151*
DATE: *17.12.1944*
PLACE: *Kargov*
EVENT: *After shootings 148/149 S. observed a Russian sniper and observer going to cover. S. shot the observer first in the head from 250 metres. In the subsequent duel with the Russian sniper, Gefr S. succeeded in eliminating him with a shot to the head.*
WITNESS: *Gefr Dubail, 5. Komp*

Whilst on the way from 7. Company command post to the forward positions at Jastrzebiec, I saw a Russian despatch runner proceeding in the open without a care in the world and shot him through the chest at 400 metres range (*152*); this was witnessed by Obergefreiter Haubensack.

CONFIRMED CLAIM: *152*
DATE: *17.12.1944*
PLACE: *Jastrzebiec*
EVENT: *On the way from 7. Company command post forward S. saw at 400 metres range a Russian despatch runner proceeding from a Russian command post into the trenches without taking cover. S. shot this Russian in the chest.*
WITNESS: *ObGefr Haubensack 7. Komp*

I observed two Russians engaged in conversation in a shallow trench forward of the farmstead that they held and looking towards our front line. One rose a little too high and I shot him in the chest (*153*). Witnesses were Haubensack and Gefreiters Matschick, Dubail and Balmers.

To mark my 150th confirmed claim I received a small packet from the C-in-C, 4. Panzer-Armee, General Gräser, who wrote to me: 'To Gefreiter Sutkus via 68. Inf Div It is with great pleasure that I have heard of your 150th confirmed claim as sniper and express to you my special recognition. I am sending you the enclosed as a souvenir. I wish you continuing success and a soldier's good fortune. Signed, Gräser, General der Panzertruppe.' The gold watch enclosed was a special form of award to successful snipers.

On the night of 17 December 1944, the Russians at the Jastrzebiec farmstead planted bushes to cover a gap in the wall through which we could view their positions. The job was botched and through an opening I saw a soldier moving about as if to keep warm and shot him through the chest at 400 metres (*154*). Next I noticed an artillery spotter correcting fire on our front line and shot him through the chest at the same range (*155*). At midday a despatch runner passed from their positions towards the command post: I could see part of his body and shot him through the chest from 400 metres (*156*). At 1530 hrs I saw several Russians moving behind the screen of bushes along the farmyard wall. In a thirty-minute period I shot two of them that were spurning adequate cover (*157*) (*158*). Range was 400 metres, and the witnesses were Unteroffiziers Kreisl, Stephan, Obergefrieter Haubensack and Grenadier Horst Büttner, 7. Company.

In recognition of my successes I was summoned to meet General der Panzertruppe Gräser. The Panzer-Armee Commander-in-Chief was very interested to hear about my training and my path to success. I had to tell him all I could about my missions. I left the command post with the gift of a hamper. It was here that I met nurse Erika Lenz for the second time. Returning to the front line I spent an hour with her, during which time she prepared me a meal.

On Christmas Eve 1944 Erika and the senior nursing sister visited the front line, bringing greetings from the homeland. The battalion CO was opposed to having them go further forward because of the danger. At this time the enemy was on the Vistula and preparing to expand his bridgehead. Bitter fighting was frequent, with constant artillery barrages. Erika asked where she could find sniper Sutkus.

When they told her, she replied, 'I must be where my sniper Bruno is!' They were forced to let her go forward whether they liked it or not. I had gone to the despatch runners' bunker to eat. Suddenly the door opened and Erika stood there. It was like a vision. She represented everything for me: homeland, life, love, everything worth living and dying for. She embraced me and kissed me. It was the best Christmas present I ever had. I will always think of her now on Christmas Eve as long as I live. I can never forget her.

In the afternoon of 27 December 1944 near Jastrzebiec, from 5. Company sector I noticed constant comings and goings behind the screen of bushes at the farmstead. I shot an officer in the chest through a gap in the bushes (*159*), range 400 metres. In the garden of the farmstead I saw two Russians carrying planks and beams to a building site. I shot them both from 400 metres (*160*) (*161*). As dusk fell, a despatch runner emerged from the trenches and gave me a clear shot to his chest from 400 metres (*162*). The witness was Gefreiter von Frieling.

In the early hours of 28 December 1944 with 5. Company I watched the Russians working on their building site in the farmstead orchard. I shot one immediately (*163*), and about thirty minutes later another Russian carrying building materials (*164*) and then another from 350 metres (*165*).

The dwellings to the right of the farmstead housed a Russian command post that received a lively traffic of despatch runners. From 350 metres at 1000 hrs I shot an incautious Russian as he walked from the orchard to the command post (*166*). Around midday the traffic of runners stepped up considerably, and I shot another from 350 metres (*167*). An infantryman must have seen my position for I came under inaccurate SMG fire. When he hopped out of his position I shot him from 350 metres (*168*). At 1500 hrs I saw a Russian leave the command post for the orchard: I had the path in my field of fire and shot him down from 350 metres (*169*).

Towards 1600 hrs I watched a Russian go from the orchard to the command post and return a short time later: I got a clear view and shot him through the chest from 350 metres (*170*). The witnesses were Uffz Kostrema, Obergrenadier Horst Arnold and Obergrenadiers Haffner, Gefreiters Max Bartel and Anton Dubail, 5. Company.

In the late afternoon of 29 December 1944 near Kargov I saw mobile sentries on the Karnickelberg. When one neglected to take cover and exposed half his body I shot him through the chest from 300 metres (**171**).

At about 0800 on 30 December 1944 I noticed an artillery spotter in the left window of the third dwelling to the right of the farmstead. From the window he could see our lines and was well positioned to direct their guns. When he ventured too far from cover I shot him in the chest from 400 metres (**172**).

CONFIRMED CLAIM: *172*

DATE: *30.10.1944*

PLACE: *Jastrzebiec*

EVENT: *Roughly towards 0800 hrs S. observed in the third house right ofthe farmstead in the left window a Russian observer who was probably directing the enemy artillery fire from there. S. shot this Russian with a shot to the chest from 400 metres.*

WITNESS: *ObGefr Arnold, 5. Komp*

In the later morning I saw a Russian heading from the command post to the bunkers. When he crossed open ground near the orchard I shot him from 300 metres (**173**).

CONFIRMED CLAIM: *173*

DATE: *30.12.1944*

PLACE: *Jastrzebiec*

EVENT: *Before noon S. espied a Russian making his way from the command post along the track to the bunker. As he crossed an open section of the orchard S. shot the Russian at 300 metres range with a shot to the chest.*

WITNESS: *ObGefr Häffner, 5. Komp*

After these successes the Russians made determined attempts to winkle me out. I had a sniper, a machine gunner and an infantryman with a sub machine gun set against me. From 5. Company trenches I saw the sniper's muzzle fire and got down just as his explosive round hit the trench wall. Lightning fast I seized the opportunity to rise, fire and hit the sniper from 300 metres (**174**). He must have fired at me again the same instant but missed.

CONFIRMED CLAIM: *174*
DATE: *30.12.1944*
PLACE: *Jastrzebiec*
EVENT: *After shot 173 the enemy attempted to take out Gefr. S. using snipers, and an SMG and MG gunner. S. saw the muzzle flash of the enemy sniper suddenly, went to ground and an explosive shell hit the trench wall. Immediately afterwards, S. stood up and shot the sniper from 300 metres. A shot fired at him the self-same moment by the Russian sniper flew wide.*
WITNESS: *OberGefr Häffner, 5. Komp*

After this duel the other two kept firing. I remained concealed and the Soviets were then distracted by one of our own machine guns, which opened fire fifty metres away from me. I waited for the SMG soldier to change position and shot him from 350 metres (**175**).

CONFIRMED CLAIM: *175*
DATE: *30.12.1944*
PLACE: *Jastrzebiec*
EVENT: *After the duel with the Russian sniper the Russian MP and MG gunners opened fire on S. S. was forced to keep down. When one of our MGs fifty metres to his left opened fire on the Russians, they were distracted and S. succeeded in shooting the MP gunner in the chest as he changed his position. Range: 350 metres.*
WITNESS: *OberGefr Häffner, 5. Komp*

The Russians were now in a furore and decided to try their luck with an anti-tank rifle. I saw the muzzle flashes and got well down. The projectiles hit and exploded, but all went well wide. Observer Gefreiter Anton Dubail crawled about fifty metres to my left and waved his cap above the trench parapet. The Russians saw this. When one rose a little to fire at the cap I shot him from 350 metres (**176**).

CONFIRMED CLAIM: *176*
DATE: *30.12.1944*
PLACE: *Jastrzebiec*
EVENT: *After the previous shots the Russians opened fire with an anti-tank rifle. S. saw the muzzle flash and took cover, the shell flew above him and hit the trench edge. Gefr Dubail, appointed observer, crawled fifty metres*

*left after some hits, raised his cap over the trench edge and deceived the*
*Russians. At that a Russian observer aimed in the direction of Dubail*
*and S. used the opportunity to shoot the Russian with shot to the chest*
*at range 350 metres.*
WITNESS: *Gefr Dubail, 5. Komp*

Returning to 5. Company command post, Uffz Eichler called me to
point out a Russian sentry in the orchard. I shot him from 600 metres
(**177**). Eichler, Häffner, Horst Arnold and Dubail were witnesses.

CONFIRMED CLAIM: *177*
DATE: *30.12.1944*
PLACE: *Jastrzebiec*
EVENT: *Passing time at the company command post, S. was summoned*
*suddenly by Uffz. Eichler. The latter drew his attention to a Russian*
*sentry standing in the orchard. S. fired at the Russian, who clutched*
*his left shoulder and collapsed. After a second shot the Russian lay*
*motionless on the ground. Range 600 metres*
WITNESS: *Uffz Eichler, 5. Komp*

I spent New Year in the Baranov bridgehead. This Soviet
bridgehead on the Vistula was a hundred kilometres long and fifty
deep. It was opposed by only two German corps, who were facing
an enormous Russian superiority in men and materials. At 0900 hrs
on 3 January 1945 near Jastrzebiec I saw a Russian leave the bunker
and enter a house. When he reappeared a short while later I shot
him in the doorway from 600 metres (**178**).

CONFIRMED CLAIM: *178*
DATE: *3.1.1945*
PLACE: *Jastrzebiec*
EVENT: *Around 0900 hrs S. observed a Russian go from the bunker into*
*a house. When the Russian was about to leave the house a short while*
*later, S. shot him in the chest at 600 metres range in the house doorway.*
WITNESS: *Gefr Bolsinger, 7. Komp*

Towards 1530 hrs the Russians went to their positions in the
farmstead orchard. One of them became half-visible behind his
MG, allowing me a successful shot from 600 metres (**179**).

CONFIRMED CLAIM: *179*
DATE: *3.1.1945*
PLACE: *Jastrzebiec*
EVENT: *Towards 1530 hrs the Russians began to occupy the trenches in the orchard. When one Russian revealed half his body above his MG, S. shot him in the chest. Range 600 metres.*
WITNESS: *Gefr Bräuer, 7. Komp*

As dusk fell towards 1600 hrs, I spotted a despatch runner sprinting from the command post to the bunkers. I shot him through the chest from 550 metres (*180*). Witnesses were Grenadier Bolsingenand, Gefreiter Bräuer from 7. Company.

In the early morning of 4 January 1945 near Przyboro I saw a Russian soldier proceeding in the open from the bunkers to the horse corral. I shot him from 600 metres (*181*). Around 0730 hrs I observed a bunker in the enemy's forward sentry position from where a Red Army man appeared at regular intervals to look around. I took him out from 500 metres with a shot to the chest (*182*). At midday I was ordered to operate near Jastrzebiec. At 1530 hrs I saw a Russian leave the bunkers and go through a communication trench towards the night trenches. I shot him from 350 metres (*183*). A second man appeared fifteen minutes later and stood by the body. I shot him also from 350 metres (*184*).

On 5 January 1945 our artillery bombarded the expanse of Russian trenches in the farmstead. During a pause in the fire some of the Russians left the trenches for the bunkers. I shot one at 400 metres (*185*). After 1500 hrs the enemy spotted me and aimed a few mortars at me. I noticed two Russians behind the bushes apparently directing the fire and shot one of these from 400 metres (*186*). Another Russian ran along the trench to observe the mortar line of fire, and as he did so I shot him (*187*). Witnesses were Haubensack and Gefreiter Martin from 7. Company.

Towards 0730 hrs on 6 January 1945 I noticed a great deal of activity in the farmstead. No doubt the Russians were happy that the prevailing conditions of fog provided good cover and they seemed carefree. When the mist lifted a little I got a view of the farmyard and shot an officer through the chest from 300 metres as he rose up from amongst a group (*188*). The weather was unchanged at 0830 hrs when I shot another Russian officer, from the same distance, who was making his way through a trench and had come to a section that had been excavated too shallowly (**189**). At 1500 hrs I observed two Russians running through the orchard towards the command post and hit one as he crossed the supply path (**190**). The other immediately went to ground but waited only a short time before resuming his run, and I shot him from 350 metres on his way to the command post (**191**). Towards 1630 hrs, after they had occupied their night trenches, I noticed two Russians standing behind a tree looking towards the German positions. I shot one from 300 metres when he strayed too far from shelter (**192**) and another thirty minutes later in a trench (**193**).

At around 1800 hrs I saw a Russian sprint from the dwellings towards the orchard. I fired but missed him. He did not seem to have noticed, for he carried on as if nothing had happened, and my second round hit him from 350 metres (**194**). My witnesses were Obergefreiter Blume and Gefreiters Völkel, Weintzek and Magus from 7. Company.

Before 0700 hrs on 7 January 1945 I saw several Russians leaving their night trenches for the dwellings. I fired twice from 400 metres and hit two of them (**195**) (**196**). After prolonged observation, towards 0800 hrs I made out a well-camouflaged Russian, probably an artillery spotter. When he stood up for a better look at our positions I shot him through the chest from 400 metres (**197**). A group of six Russians left the orchard and headed for the bunkers through a communication trench. I shot the leading man (**198**). The others wanted to carry his body with them, which gave me a second opportunity, and I shot another soldier from 350 metres (**199**). As a result of these two successes I was seen and fired on by a sniper. I saw his muzzle flash, ducked my head and the bullet hit the trench parapet. I sent one of our men with a lure to my right. When he raised it above the parapet, the enemy sniper fired at it immediately. In order to obtain a better field of fire the Soviet sniper undertook a change of position. I shot him from 300 metres – my 200th success.

CONFIRMED CLAIM: *200*
DATE: *7.1.1945*
PLACE: *Jastrzebiec*
EVENT: *After the previous shots S. was fired upon by a Russian sniper.*

S. sent a sentry to his right to deceive the opponent. This sentry raised a
lure over the trench parapet, and the Russian fired at it. As the Russian
sniper had no field of fire he came right. S. then shot him from 300 metres.
WITNESS: *ObGefr Völkel, 7. Komp*

At 1100 hrs a group of about nine Russians came from the
orchard towards their forward trenches, led by an officer. When
they arrived at the bodies of victims 198 and 199, whom I had
shot dead two hours previously, they left the trench, presumably
because they did not want to have to clamber over the corpses. This
was a very favourable situation for me and I shot six, one after the
other (*201*) (*202*) (*203*) (*204*) (*205*) (*206*).

In 7. Company front sector at about 1530 hrs I noticed a Russian
proceeding from the trenches to the bunkers. I shot him through
the chest from 400 metres (*207*). My witnesses were Obergefreiters
Völkel and Dietze, and Gefreiter Kracht.

CONFIRMED CLAIM: *207*
DATE: *7.1.1945*
PLACE: *Jastrzebiec*
EVENT: *Towards 1530 hrs S. saw a Russian going from the trenches to the
bunker. He was shot by S. from 400 metres range.*
WITNESS: *Gefr Kracht, 7. Komp*

On 9 January 1945 I watched the Russian forward observers
returning to their positions. I succeeded in hitting one of them from
500 metres (*208*). Towards 1530 hrs I saw several Russians emerge
from the bunker and make their way through the orchard to the
forward trenches. I shot one of them in the chest from 300 metres
(*209*). The witnesses were Obergefreiter Kleber and Gefreiter
Martin, 7. Company.

After this long period of trench warfare it was becoming evident
that the Russians were about to make a move, and everything
pointed to a major offensive. Their trenches now held double the
number of troops compared to the average we had seen before.

I had caught a chill and developed a high fever. I was sent to the
rear to see a doctor in the nearby village where our field hospital
was located. Even there, one sensed the tension – something was
in the offing. It had been arranged for the C-in-C, 4. Panzer-Armee,

General Gräser, to throw a small party for me at the *Soldatenheim* on 12 March 1945. It had been the intention of Erika Lenz and myself to announce our engagement at the same time. I was ordered by 5. Company to report to Major Hoffmann at Battalion Staff. The regimental adjutant, Hauptmann Schöpphagen, who had written the OKH newspaper article about me in October, congratulated me on my promotion to Obergefreiter – senior corporal. My sojourn at the front had come to an end, I was being seconded to Sniper School as an instructor. Major Hoffmann regretted the loss of his best sniper.

I was asleep when an artillery bombardment rained down on the German trenches at 0300 hrs on the morning of 12 January. The earth trembled with the shock. The Russians had reinforced their Vistula bridgehead and two armies were now bent on the break out. In eight hours, 800,000 shells fell on a single square kilometre. The fire was fearsome. At 0800 hrs everything fell quiet and loudspeakers on the Russian side of the front played music. This accompanied an offer that they had declared a half-hour truce so that those of our men who wished to do so could lay down their arms and cross over. The Red Army would guarantee that whoever did so would return home after the war had ended. On the other hand, should we ignore this opportunity, the Russians would resume their barrage and kill all of us 'Fascist dogs' without mercy. Nobody from II Battalion/Gren Regt 196 defected – everybody stayed in their trench.

At 0830 hrs on the dot their artillery resumed. A hurricane of shells of all calibres came hurtling down on us. Billows of dust and smoke darkened the battlefield. Enemy tanks trundled towards our positions. We received the order to disengage and fall back on the reserve trenches to limit our casualties. A shell exploded near me and wounded my left hand. It was very painful; it turned a nasty colour and swelled up. Fortunately it was not shattered.

At 1030 hrs the Russians increased their range to knock out our guns to the rear. Then they advanced, seven ranks of infantry shoulder to shoulder, one rank behind another. Two hundred tanks rolled towards our trenches. Our infantry, already stunned by the artillery bombardment, was no match for such an overwhelmingly superior enemy. The Luftwaffe, which ought to have nipped the Russian preparations in the bud, was never seen. Shortage of fuel kept the available German fighters on the ground.

We were faced with no alternative but to pull back or be steamrollered to destruction. Passing through our artillery positions, a battery commander, pistol drawn, forced us to occupy his defensive trenches in the effort to cover the withdrawal of his guns. Chaos reigned, it was everybody for himself.

On 19 January 1945 I crawled into a house. My wounded hand looked awful. A shell landed and buried me alive. Comrades dragged me free and carried me unconscious to a central dressing station where my hand underwent surgery. From there I was taken to the field hospital at Gleiwitz in Silesia. On 22 January I handed in my sniper rifle at the arsenal and received a receipt.

As the Russians bore down on the Lithuanian–German border the German populace was evacuated. My parents finished up at Stöblitz/Rochlitz outside Leipzig. As they knew my field post number they could write to me at the Gleiwitz hospital. Once the Russians approached Gleiwitz we wounded were transported out by rail. When my train reached Rochlitz I alighted and was directed to the reserve hospital at Burgstädt. By now my hand looked so bad that the doctors wanted to amputate; I refused. I also had pains on the left side of my chest, and had been spitting blood since being buried. I received more treatment. At the Burgstädt hospital a letter and parcel arrived for me. On 11 January 1945 General Gräser, C-in-C, 4. Panzer-Armee, wrote to mark my 207th confirmed claim:

To Gefreiter Bruno Sutkus, Staff, Grenadier Regiment 196. With great pleasure I learnt of your 207th success. I know what courage, endurance and devotion to duty allied to masterly skill enabled you to make this outstanding achievement. In doing so you have caused the enemy significant losses, and to your comrades you are a shining example of single-minded readiness to fight. Therefore I express to you my special recognition and send you a parcel for your personal use. Heil Hitler! Signed Gräser, General der Panzertruppe.

Here in the hospital at Burgstädt the wounded had to be carried down to the air raid cellars whenever the alarm sounded. This was bad enough, but far better than holding out in the trenches under direct enemy artillery fire, in rain, snow and cold. On 1 March 1945 the chief surgeon awarded me the Wound badge in silver for my third combat injury.

~

# German Publisher's Note

These are Bruno Sutkus's decorations and awards: 6.7.1944 Iron Cross 2. Class; 7.9.1944 Wound badge in black, 16.11.1944 Iron Cross 1. Class; 21.11.1944 Sniper Proficiency Badge, Grade 3; 25.11.1944 Mentioned in *Wehrmacht Report*; 29.11.1944 Infantry Assault Badge in silver; 1.3.1945 Wound badge in silver.

When one considers Sutkus's successes and compares them with the sniper successes in other Divisions, there is no doubt that he belongs in the very top rank of snipers of the German Wehrmacht. In order to clarify this comparison, we must look at original documents containing the claims of snipers from these other Divisions.

(1)   I/SS Panzer Grenadier Regiment 6 *Theodor Eicke* of 3. Panzer Division *Totenkopf*: Gerd Klopp with seventeen and Erich Mattern with twenty-five claims in the autumn of 1944 were amongst the most successful snipers. (See divisional newspaper *Totenkopf Melder*, November 1944.)

(2)   In February 1945, SS-Unterscharführer Kühn of 17. Panzer Grenadier Division *Götz von Berlichingen* was named the most successful sniper on the Western Front with twenty confirmed claims (divisional newspaper *Die Eiserne Front*, February 1945).

(3)   Amongst the most successful snipers of 23. SS Freiwilligen Panzer Grenadier Division *Nederland* was SS-Unterscharführer Steinke, who obtained his twenty-sixth confirmed claim in Kurland on 12 January 1945. (War Diary, SS Panzer Grenadier Brigade/Nederland).

(4)   In the sniper platoon of the SS-Jagdverbände, SS-Rottenführer Scheffel and SS-Sturmmann Beuckels had each achieved sixty confirmed claims by March 1945. (Oderkorps Daily Report, 21 March

1945). All snipers mentioned above may have increased their tally of successes by the last weeks of the war, but would certainly not have scored 210 successes by then to better Sutkus.

(5)   Knight's Cross holder Gefreiter Matthäus Hetzenauer is recognised in wartime records as the most successful German Wehrmacht sniper with 345 confirmed claims.

Reichsführer-SS Heinrich Himmler constantly drew attention to sniper successes and encouraged them. After he became C-in-C of the *Ersatzheer* in 1944, he raised the Volksgrenadier Divisions in the Army, and sniper successes achieved by the Waffen-SS and the Army's Volksgrenadier were published by him in his Daily Orders. Himmler had recognised that successful snipers were at a disadvantage when it came to decorations. He wanted to change this so as to have the achievements of front-line soldiers acknowledged much sooner, and to motivate snipers to greater success.

Accordingly, the Reichsführer-SS made it known that for one hundred confirmed claims the sniper concerned would be recommended for the German Cross in Gold. Himmler's announcement also stated:

> Grenadiers are the true carriers of battle. Amongst them, the sniper stands out above all. Special recognition will be paid to his efforts:
>
> For five confirmed claims by soldiers not trained as snipers: Mention in Divisional Daily Orders and five days' special leave, together with transfer as sniper trainee.
>
> For ten confirmed claims: Seven days' special leave, Iron Cross 2. Class, Mention in Divisional Daily Orders.
>
> For twenty confirmed claims: Sniper Proficiency Badge, Grade 1.
>
> For thirty confirmed claims: fourteen days' special leave, Mention in Corps Daily Orders.
>
> For forty confirmed claims: Sniper proficency badge, Grade 2.
>
> For fifty confirmed claims: twenty days' special leave, Iron Cross 1. Class, Mention in Army Daily Orders.
>
> For sixty confirmed claims: Sniper Proficiency Badge, Grade 3.
>
> For one hundred confirmed claims: recommendation for the German Cross in Gold.
>
> The divisional commander will decide in every case on the special leave to be awarded. The sniper with 150 confirmed claims will be summoned to appear before the Reichsführer-SS in person. His

name will appear in the Reichsführer-SS Daily Orders for the entire Waffen-SS and Volksgrenadier Divisions.

(Divisional newspaper, 17. SS-Panzer-Grenadier-Div *Götz von Berlichingen*, *'Die Eiserne Faust'*, February 1945).

From the foregoing it will be seen that Himmler intended to link the award of decorations for bravery to confirmed claims. On this basis, after one hundred confirmed successes, a sniper was to be recommended for the award of the German Cross in Gold by his regimental CO.

If Bruno Sutkus had been with a Volksgrenadier Division of the Army or the Waffen-SS, he would possibly have been recommended for the German Cross in Gold, and after his 200th confirmed claim the equivalent of the bar, or *Ehrenblatt* clasp, or perhaps the award of the Knight's Cross. Ultimately this must remain conjecture. In Sutkus's case, various statements have been made regarding a recommendation that he should receive the award of the Knight's Cross, but these remain unconfirmed.

Undoubtedly it must be thought odd that Bruno Sutkus was not considered for a major bravery award even though his Division, Corps and Army were constantly informed as to the number of his successes, as this book clearly shows. It was the responsibility of Sutkus's competent battalion CO, to whom he was directly accountable, to submit the recommendation. If this was not done because of the constant defensive predicament in which the Division found itself, or a recommendation was submitted but got lost in the communication channels, this is something that can no longer be determined.

The only high distinction he received, but which he could not wear outwardly, was the mention of the name Bruno Sutkus in the German *Wehrmacht Report* of 25 November 1944. For this alone he will be known in German war history.

1   Bruno Sutkus, autumn 1944. The optic is the 4-power Zeiss Ajack telescopic sight graduated to 1,200 metres.

2  (Top) German heavy artillery replying to a Soviet attack in the Carpathians.
(Bottom) German MG 42 machine-gun nest.

3    A German sniper with the high turret ZF-K98k rifle sighted to 1,200 metres.

4    (Top Left) General der Panzertruppe Fritz-Hubert Gräser, C-in-C, 4. Panzer-Armee, who expressed his admiration of Sutkus's skills in several letters of recognition. Gräser held the Knight's Cross with Oak Leaves and Swords. (Top Right) Generalmajor Paul Scheuerpflug, GOC, 68. Inf Div, received the Oak Leaves to his Knight's Cross and was promoted to Generalleutnant with effect from 16 March 1945. He died under Soviet administration in the former concentration camp at Auschwitz on 8 August 1945. (Bottom) A sniper pair in action.

5   The conflict on the Eastern Front in 1944 made the greatest demands and sacrifices of all fighting men.

Die vom Oberkommando des Heeres herausgegebene Zeitung „Unser Heer" veröffentlichte am 1. Oktober 1944 einen großen Bericht über den Scharfschützen Bruno Sutkus.

bis zur Mitte der im Niemandsland verlaufenden Rollbahn vorgetrieben, um sich so einen Ausgangspunkt für Spähtruppunternehmen zu schaffen. Das Handwerk konnte dem Burschen nicht gelegt werden, da sie sich im Schutze der überhöhten Rollbahn bewegten und vor einem überraschenden Zugreifen durch unseren eigenen Minengürtel gesichert waren. Das war also eine Aufgabe für unseren Scharfschützen. Im Graben war allgemeine Spannung. Wird er es schaffen? Es kam auf sekundenschnelles Erfassen und blitzschnelles Handeln an. Da, eben waren ganz kurz ein paar Hände mit einem Spaten zu sehen! Lieber Iwan, jetzt hat er dich weg, nur noch eine kleine Unvorsichtigkeit, und du wirst dein Tun teuer bezahlen müssen!

Reglos verharrt unser Scharfschütze hinter seinem Gewehr. Auch der Feind ist ebenfalls aufmerksam und bewacht unseren Graben. Seine Züge sind angespannt, die Nerven und Muskeln dürfen nicht erlahmen. Der Ostpreuße mit seiner sprichwörtlichen Ruhe garantiert, daß ihm der entscheidende Augenblick nicht entgehen wird. Die Zeit schleicht dahin. Immer wieder kommt hochgeworfene Erde zum Vorschein. Der Gegner ist doch vorsichtig, er gibt sich keine Blöße.

Da kracht ein Schuß! Nur für eine Sekunde hat der Iwan sich gestreckt und hat über den Graben gekommen. Das hat genügt, der Kopfschuß war tödlich. Der im Graben mit beobachtende Gruppenführer dankt dem Kameraden mit festem Händedruck.

Am anderen Abend. — Mit Beginn der Dämmerung schoben sich die Sowjets jeden Abend an die Rollbahn vor. Jetzt etwa müßten sie wieder erscheinen. Zunächst war nicht festzustellen, in welcher Stärke sie den Abschnitt besetzten. Sie begannen mit ihrer Arbeit, während unser Beobachtungsposten bezog. Schemenhaft waren nur ab und an huschende Schatten im Gewirr des Unterholzes wie Waldgeister mehr zu denken als zu erkennen. Da mußte schon ein ausgezeichnetes Glas die Spukgestalten heranholen. Aber erst in Verbindung mit einer sehr ruhigen und sicheren Hand wäre vielleicht ein Abschuß einer solchen Schottengestalt möglich.

Das war also wieder so recht eine Aufgabe für

unseren Scharfschützen. — Aufmerksam verfolgt er die Bewegungen des schanzenden Feindes. Fest prägt er sich den Standort ein. Denn schon nach jedem Absetzen des Glases muß er erneut den Punkt in dem sich überall gleichenden Waldrand suchen. Jetzt umfaßt er sein Gewehr und nimmt den Gegner aufs Korn. Er bleibt im Ziel. Aber immer wieder verschwindet die Gestalt, die unbedingt im Zieldreieck des Glases verharren muß. Wie oft setzt der Finger krümmend an und kommt nicht zum Durchziehen, weil inzwischen im Ziel nur noch das Astgewirr zu sehen ist.

Geduldsprobe! Wer kennt nicht die vielen Spottsprüche über die Engelsgeduld eines Anglers! In noch schärferem Maße muß die Geduld bei einem Scharfschützen ausgeprägt sein. Denn sein Wild beißt nicht an und es kann auch nicht geködert werden.

Jetzt krümmt sich der Finger wieder. Schuß! — Vornüber fällt die braune Gestalt auf die von ihr selbst geschaufelte Erde. Ein dahinter schanzender Genosse will sich um den Toten oder einen dest Schwerverletzten kümmern. Vorsichtig kommt er heran. Zaudernd betritt er die unheilvolle Stätte. Wie kann man sich so tölpelhaft im Ge-

fahrenbereich eines Scharfschützen bewegen. Zu spät geht er in die bereits aufgeworfene Deckung. Schon war sein Schatten im Zieldreieck des Scharfschützenglases, und mit dem verhallenden Schuß sinkt der zweite Gegner auf den kühlen Waldboden.

Und am nächsten Tage! Noch tropft es in dicken Wassertropfen aus dem Laubdach des Bataillonswaldes, von wo aus sich der Gefreite S. im Morgengrauen zu den Stellungen der 5. Kompanie in Marsch setzt. Heute führt er Krieg auf eigene Faust. Der Anstand im Stellungssystem und das Warten auf heraustretende Feinde liegt ihm heute nicht. Er will den Feind im eigenen Bau aufspüren.

Langsam und vorsichtig nach allen Seiten lugend schiebt er sich hinter den Graben, mit ihm zur Sicherung der Gruppenführer dieses Abschnitts und ein weiterer beherzter Mann. Das Ziel ist die Waldschneise im Feindwald jenseits der Rollbahn. Meter um Meter gleiten sie durch die schmale Gasse der Minensperre und robben ungeachtet des Lehmbreies über die Rollbahn.

Jetzt kommt das Wagnis, der Sprung in die Höhle des Löwen, in den Wald. Mit einigem Pech hätten sie gerade einen feindlichen Posten in die Arme springen können. Zu einem solchen Unternehmen gehört schon ein bißchen Glück. Die Waldschneise ist erreicht. Gefreiter Sutkus fühlt sich langsam an den Rand vor und äugt zwischen den Hochwaldstämmen den Weg entlang. So vorsichtig ist das alles geschehen, daß der sowjetische Posten, der in einiger Entfernung zwischen den Stämmen an der anderen Seite der Schneise steht, nichts wahrgenommen hat.

Gewehr hoch, in aller Ruhe gezielt und abgedrückt! Lautlos sinkt der Posten zwischen zwei Bäumen zusammen. Mäuschenstill verhalten sich unsere drei Späher. Wer weiß, wie viele Augenpaare sich jetzt in das Vorfeld bohren. In zweiter Bolschewist kommt, um nach seinem Genossen zu sehen. Er überquert die Schneise und läuft direkt in die Schußbahn. Im letzten Schritt bricht er zusammen.

Die Beute ist gut! Vorsichtig, die Augen am Feind, treten die drei Pirschgänger entlang der Waldschneise den Rückweg an. Da vernehmen sie

von links herüben das Sprechen im 160... fernung wird ein sieben Mann starker Spähtrupp sichtbar. Ein Glück, daß die Kerle durch ihr Geschwätz verraten haben! Ein erkannter Gegner bedeutet keine Gefahr mehr für solche beherzten Männer. Sutkus nimmt das Maschinengewehrschützen aufs Korn und läßt ihn einem Kopfschuß umfallen. Das Überraschungsmoment wird ausgenützt, um die von dem eigenen Posten überwachte Hauptkampflinie zu erreichen. Der feindliche Spähtrupp ist leichtsinnig genug, weiter vorzugehen, um durch die Baumsperre einen Blick ins Vorgelände zu werfen.

Eine Scharte in der Sperre genügt für unseren geübten Scharfschützen. Mit ruhiger Sicherheit sucht er sich den durch seine besondere Kleidung auffallenden Führer des Spähtrupps, der den Ausrüstung nach ein Offizier sein muß, heraus. Den Blick ins Niemandsland endet ein wohlgezielter Kopfschuß für immer.

So ist unser Scharfschütze zu einem unentbehrlichen Helfer der Kameraden vorn im Graben geworden. Zäh und verbissen in stundenlanger Ausdauer hat er mit jedem seiner wohlgezielten Schüsse viel Kameradenblut gespart.

# Alle Achtung vor Sutkus!

## EIN KAMERAD BERICHTET AUS DEM VORDERSTEN GRABEN

In seiner dreckverschmierten Tarnbekleidung steht der eben aus der Stellung kommende Scharfschütze, Gefreiter Sutkus aus Fichtenhöhe (Kr. Schloßberg), vor seinem Kommandeur und empfängt aus dessen Hand das Eiserne Kreuz. Damit wurden ungezählte gefahrvolle Einzeleinsätze belohnt, die nur den nächsten Beteiligten bekannt sind. Sie haben dem Gegner empfindliche Verluste beigebracht. Ein Kamerad erzählt von den Erfolgen dieses Scharfschützen im vordersten Graben:

Vor dem linken Abschnitt der 7. Kompanie eines Grenadierregiments hatten die Bolschewisten in nächtelanger Wühlarbeit einen Stichgraben fast

## Ich bestätige...

### AUFGABEN UND ERFOLGE UNSERER SCHARFSCHÜTZEN

2

6    The newspaper *Unser Heer*, issued by OKH, published a long article on Bruno Sutkus in the 1 October 1944 edition. A translation appears in the text on pages 15–16 and 19–22.

7   A German soldier hugs cover in a forward trench under fire.

**...er Tageblatt**

...ageblatt / Lokalblatt für Wechselburg — Enthält Bekanntmachungen der Bürgermeister zu Rochlitz, Geringswalde und anderer Behörden

...nd Sonntag, den 25./26. November 1944 — Geschäftsstelle Geringswalde: Bahnhofstr. 14 — Fernsprecher Nr. 15 — 125. Jahrg.

# Abwehrschlacht bei Aachen vor dem Höhepunkt

### ...pfe im Hochwald von Hürtgen — Voller deutscher Abwehrerfolg in Kurland
### Deutsche Besatzung von Sworbe auf das Festland übergeführt

...s dem Führerhauptquartier, 25. Nov. ...
...mando der Wehrmacht gibt bekannt:

...hrschlacht bei Aachen nähert sich ihrem Höhe... ...änzung ihrer schweren Verluste führten gestern ...aner im Raum zwischen Geilenkirchen und Esch... ...äfte aus der Tiefe heran und versuchten ihre... ...ungen für die Fortsetzung der Angriffe zu ... ...e Divisionen zersprengten Panzeransammlungen ...engefaßtes Artilleriefeuer und warfen den Feind ...en zurück. Im Hochwald bei Hürtgen verfing sich ...er nordamerikanische Angriffe in schweren Wald...

...mpfgruppen setzten im Raum von Metz ihren ...n den alten Forts fort.

...and nordöstlich des Bischwaldes in Ost-Lothringen ...ahlreiche feindliche Angriffe. Gegenangriffe unserer ...en nördlich Saarburg den feindlichen Bewegungen ...aber in die Flanke.

...Stadt Straßburg und ihrem Umkreis verteidigten ...ppen in älteren Werken und Befestigungsanlagen. ...ebirgskamm der mittleren Vogesen haben sich ...pfe entwickelt.

...ruppen im Ober-Elsaß kämpften den größten ...ttes hart vom Feinde frei und dringen in breiter ...Westen und Südwesten vor.

...Belfort hält dem starken Druck des Feindes auf ...e Grenze an. Entlastungsangriffe gegen unseren ...nordöstlich Delle und Ausbruchsversuche des ...Feindes scheiterten. An der Burgundischen Pforte ...t dem 16. November nach bisherigen Meldungen ...he Panzer vernichtet.

...London und Antwerpen wurde bei Tag und Nacht ...der Großraum von Lüttich verstärkt mit unseren ...offen beschossen.

...lischen Apennin griffen nordamerikanische Ver... ...e Bergstellungen südwestlich Bergeto vergeblich an. ...änze und Forli gerichteten unsere Truppen auch ...mit gewaltigem Materialeinsatz geführten Durch... ...he Divisionen nach schweren, ...über anhaltenden Kämpfen.

...setzten die Bolschewisten mit starken ...aus den Brückenköpfen bei Apatin und ...ich an. Im zusammengefaßten Abwehr...

...er kamen sie schon nach kurzem Vordrängen wieder zum ...eben.

In Mittel-Ungarn wurde hart südlich Budapest erbittert ...gekämpft. An den Brennpunkten der Abwehrschlacht blieben ...im Raum Hatvan und beiderseits Mistolc erneute starke feind... ...he Angriffe bis auf unbedeutenden Geländegewinn erfolglos.

Nordwestlich Ungvar und an der Dukla-Paß-Straße bra... ...chen örtliche Angriffe der Bolschewisten vor unseren Stel... ...lungen zusammen.

In der zweiten großen Abwehrschlacht in Kurland er... ...rangen unsere tapferen Verbände gegen den Ansturm von acht ...Sowjetarmeen einen vollen Abwehrsieg. Der nach einer Artil... ...lerievorbereitung von fast 200 000 Schuß mit zahlreichen Pan... ...zern angestrebte Durchbruch der Bolschewisten wurde, teilweise ...im Gegenangriff, abgeschlagen, geringfügige Einbrüche beseitigt.

Der Kampf auf der Halbinsel Sworbe ist beendet. Die in ...den Südteil der Halbinsel gedrängte tapfere Besatzung wurde ...im Laufe des gestrigen Tages bei dauernder Abwehr vielfach ...überlegener Angriffe der Sowjets durch Verbände der Kriegs... ...marine und Landungspioniere auf das Festland übergeführt.

Feindliche Störflugzeuge warfen in der vergangenen Nacht ...verstreut Bomben in verschiedenen Teilen des Reichsgebietes.

### Besonders ausgezeichnet

Ergänzend zum Wehrmachtsbericht wird gemeldet:

In den sieben Wochen andauernden Kämpfen um die Insel ...Oesel und den letzten Gefechten auf Sworbe haben sich Siche... ...rungsverbände der Kriegsmarine unter Führung von Fre... ...gattenkapitän Brauneis und Korvettenkapitän Kiefer ...beim Schutz der Küste durch erfolgreiche Abwehr überlegener ...sowjetischer Seestreitkräfte ausgezeichnet. Besondere Anerken... ...nungen verdienten hierbei die seemännischen Leistungen der Be... ...satzungen unserer Kampffähren und Räumboote unter Füh... ...rung des Chefs der 9. Sicherungsdivision, Fregattenkapitän ...von Blanc.

Bei den schweren Kämpfen im Brückenkopf Apatin hat sich ...das III. Bataillon des zweiten Regiments „Brandenburg" ...unter Führung von Hauptmann Heyne besonders ausge... ...zeichnet.

Der Scharfschütze Gefreiter Sutkus im Grenadier-Regi... ...ment 196 hat innerhalb von 5 Monaten 125 Gegner abge... ...schossen.

8    The *Wehrmacht Report* of 25 November 1944 mentioned Bruno Sutkus by name.

9   Bruno Sutkus with German Red Cross nurse Erika Lenz in December 1944. He has dismounted the sight from his ZF-K98k rifle; the forward mounting for this can be clearly seen.

10   Grenadier Bruno Sutkus, wearing the ribbon of the Iron Cross 2. Class, March 1945.

**Raupe und Rad** — frontzeitung nach vorn!

NACHRICHTENBLATT EINER PANZERARMEE

Nr. 470 — Dienstag, 5. Dezember 1944

# Aus unserem Kampfraum

## Das ist Sutkus!

Der Scharfschütze Obergefreiter Bruno Sutkus wurde anlässlich seines 125. Abschusses in der Ergänzung zum Wehrmachtbericht vom 25. November 1944 genannt. Ueber den Kameraden Sutkus, der Angehöriger eines Grenadier-Regiments unserer Panzer-Armee ist, geht uns folgender interessanter Bericht zu:

Seit etwa einem halben Jahr gehört er zu uns. Zuerst hielten wir ja absolut nicht viel von ihm. Gewiss, er war ein feiner Kerl, ein Kamerad wie jeder andere auch, er hatte jedoch nichts an sich, was besonders an ihm auffiel. Selbst als er seinem Bataillons-adjutanten einmal — es waren gerade wenige Tage vergangen, als er mit der letzten Ersatzzuteilung eingetroffen war — auf dessen anerkennende Worte über den ostpreussischen Soldaten abschliessend antwortete: „Jawoll, Herr Leutnant, stur wie die Panzer!" war das nichts besonderes, Ostpreussen möchten er sein.

Erst als er dann, an den Schwerpunkten des Bataillons eingesetzt, innerhalb kürzester Zeit zehn — zwanzig — dreissig, ja vierzig und sogar fünfzig Abschüsse erzielte, wurden wir auf ihn aufmerksam. Donnerwetter — das war doch allerhand. Das hatten wir die.... eigentlich bescheidenen und unscheinbaren ostpreussischen Forsfgehilfen nie zugetraut.

Die Anerkennung blieb natürlich nicht aus. Sein General, der ihn nach seinem dreissigsten Abschuss bereits mit einer Sonderzuteilung

an Schokolade auszeichnete und von da ab regen Anteil an seinen Erfolgen nahm, verlieh ihm nach seinem fünfzigsten Abschuß das Eiserne Kreuz 2. Klasse. Nach weiteren zwanzig Abschüssen traf die Anerkennung des Kommandierenden Generals in Form einer Urkunde für ihn ein.

Die Geschichte seines 100. bis 102. Abschusses jedoch verdient, besonders erwähnt zu werden. Es kam, so:

Sutkus hatte den 99. Iwan abgeschossen. Es war ausgerechnet ein sowjetischer Scharfschütze, der ihn auf dem Wege vom Bataillon zur Kompanie beschoss und in Deckung zwang. Sutkus schoss ihn, als sein Gegner kurz danach Stellungswechsel machen wollte, so im Vorbeigehen ab. Infolge eines Versehens wurde dieser Abschuss als 100. Abschuss vom Bataillon und Regiment weitergemeldet. Vom Regiment natürlich mit entsprechender Betonung: „Da könnt Ihr mal sehen, was wir für einen Scharfschützen haben." Kurz darauf wurden auch schon die Unterlagen zur Verleihung des Eisernen Kreuzes I. Klasse angefordert. Das war nun eine peinliche Sache — der Irrtum hatte sich inzwischen herausgestellt: es waren noch keine hundert! — Dem Bataillon wurde dringend empfohlen, Sutkus bis zum Morgen des nächsten Tages noch einen Iwan abschiessen zu lassen. Wie — das konnte das Regiment auch nicht sagen. Mit gemischten Gefühlen ging man schlafen. Am nächsten Morgen ein zaghafter Anruf: „Hat Sutkus vielleicht doch noch . . . .?" Eine Minute Schweigen bei der Gegenstelle. Gespannte Erwartung und Ungeduld des Anrufenden, dann erklingt die betont gedehnte Stimme des Bataillons-Kommandeurs: „Tja — wissen Sie, mein Guter, wir haben Sutkus mal eben vor die Tür geschickt. Da hat er sich gerade seinen 100. bis 102. Abschuss geholt!"

Das ist Sutkus!

Oblt. Schöppenthau.

# Führerbefehle

**34. Befehl des Führers über die Einführung eines Scharfschützenabzeichens.**

Der Führer.                                    F. H. Qu., den 20. 8. 1944.

### 1.

In Anerkennung des hohen Einsatzes des Einzelschützen mit Gewehr als Scharfschütze und zur Würdigung der hierbei erzielten Erfolge führe ich für das Heer und die ƒƒ-Verfügungstruppe das Scharfschützenabzeichen ein.

Das Scharfschützenabzeichen wird in 3 Stufen verliehen.

### 2.

Die Durchführungsbestimmungen erläßt der Gen. d. Inf. b. Chef Gen. St. d. H.

**Adolf Hitler**

---

Durchführungsbestimmungen zum Führerbefehl vom 20. 8. 1944 über die Einführung eines Scharfschützenabzeichens.

Der Führer hat ein Scharfschützenabzeichen für das Heer und die ƒƒ-Verfügungstruppe eingeführt. Hierdurch soll der hohe Einsatz des Schützen mit Gewehr und seine Erfolge im gezielten Einzelschuß gewürdigt und gleichzeitig ein Ansporn für eine Steigerung der bisher erzielten Leistungen gegeben werden. Dementsprechend ist das Scharfschützenabzeichen nach folgenden Grundsätzen zu verleihen:

1. Das Scharfschützenabzeichen wird durch den nächsten truppendienstlichen Vorgesetzten mit den Befugnissen mindestens eines Regimentskommandeurs auf schriftlichen Vorschlag des Einheitsführers an solche Soldaten verliehen, die als planmäßige Scharfschützen ausgebildet und eingesetzt sind. Dem Beliehenen ist eine Urkunde über die Verleihung auszustellen und die Verleihung in die Personalpapiere einzutragen (siehe Anlage 2).

2. Das Abzeichen (siehe Anlage 1) ist in 3 Stufen unterteilt und wird auf dem rechten Unterarm getragen. Sofern ein Soldat ein Funktionsdienstgradabzeichen besitzt oder neben dem Scharfschützenabzeichen verliehen bekommt, ist dieses unter dem Scharfschützenabzeichen zu tragen.

3. Es werden verliehen:

   Die 1. Stufe für mindestens 20 Feindabschüsse, die ab 1. 9. 1944 erzielt wurden (Abzeichen ohne besondere Umrandung);

   die 2. Stufe für mindestens 40 Feindabschüsse, die ab 1. 9. 1944 erzielt wurden (Abzeichen mit Silberkordel umrandet);

   die 3. Stufe für mindestens 60 Feindabschüsse, die ab 1. 9. 1944 erzielt wurden (Abzeichen mit goldgelber Kordel umrandet).

   Im Nahkampf erzielte Abschüsse werden nicht angerechnet. Im übrigen muß der Feind bewegungsunfähig geschossen sein und darf nicht die Absicht gezeigt haben, überzulaufen oder sich gefangen zu geben.

4. Über jeden Abschußerfolg ist bei der Einheit eine Meldung und Bestätigung durch mindestens 1 Zeugen einzureichen. Die Einheiten legen auf Grund der Meldungen Scharfschützenlisten gemäß anliegendem Muster an (Anlage 3). Ein Auszug aus der Scharfschützenliste ist bei Versetzungen der neuen Einheit zusammen mit den sonstigen Papieren zu übergeben. Eine rückwirkende Anrechnung von Abschüssen erfolgt nicht, um unnötigen Schriftverkehr zu vermeiden. Es wird vielmehr vorgeschlagen, die bisherigen Leistungen durch die Truppe bei der Verleihung von Eisernen Kreuzen mit bewerten zu lassen.

O. K. H., 20. 8. 1944
Gen. d. Inf. b/Chef Gen. St. d. H.

---

Zusatzbestimmungen des O. K. L. (LP) zum Führerbefehl vom 20. 8. 1944 über die Einführung des Scharfschützenabzeichens.

1. Laut O. K. W., 29 b 28. 14/9215/44 WZA/WZ III c, vom 14. 12. 1944 hat der Führer entschieden, daß das Scharfschützenabzeichen den im Erdkampf eingesetzten Soldaten aller Wehrmachtteile verliehen werden kann, wenn die Voraussetzungen für die Verleihung erfüllt sind.

2. Im Bereich der Luftwaffe erfolgt die Verleihung des Scharfschützenabzeichens auf Vorschlag des Einheitsführers durch den nächsten truppendienstlichen Vorgesetzten mit den Befugnissen mindestens eines Geschwaderkommodore bzw. Regimentskommandeurs. In Zweifelsfällen ist Entscheidung bei O. K. L. (LP) zu beantragen.

3. Die vorstehend bekanntgegebenen Durchführungsbestimmungen des Gen. d. Inf. b. Chef Gen. St. d. H. gelten in vollem Umfange auch für die Luftwaffe.

4. Besitzzeugnisse gemäß Anlage 2 sind von den Verleihungsdienststellen selbst zu beschaffen.

5. Der Bedarf an Abzeichen ist auf dem Bekleidungsnachschubwege zu decken. Anforderungen sind an das örtlich zuständige Luftgaukommando (Verwaltung) zu richten.

O. K. L., 2. 1. 1945,
Az. 29 g 10/LP Ausz. u. Diszpl. (I A).

L. V. Bl. S. 28

---

12    The *Führerbefehl* (Führer-Order) instituting the Sniper Proficiency Badge in three grades. A full translation of the text appears on pages 40–1.

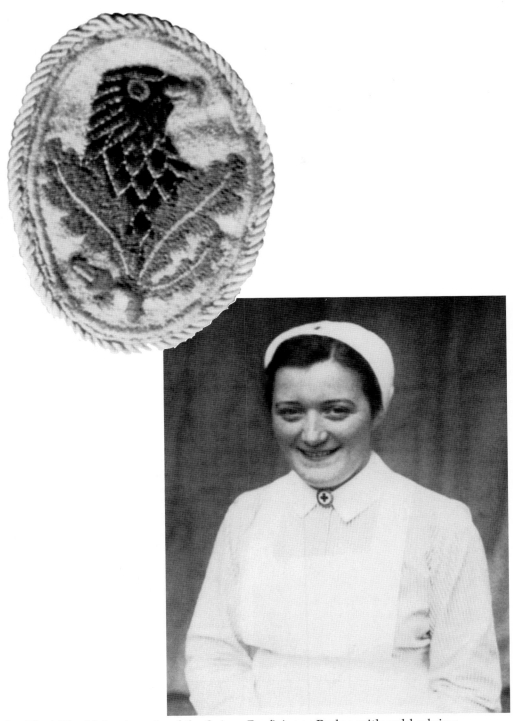

13 (Top) The highest grade of the Sniper Proficiency Badge with gold edging.
(Bottom) German Red Cross nurse Erika Lenz first met Sutkus on the Vistula in 1944
and remained in touch with him during the decades of his banishment in the Soviet
Union.

14   (Top) A work party from the Scherenkov coal mine, Sutkus kneeling at the rear. (Centre) The author during his banishment to eastern Siberia, 1960. (Bottom) At Leketschai in Lithuania at the grave of his father (d.1960).

15   In Soviet forced exile. Bruno Sutkus worked in the Siberian coal mines as a miner from 1957 to 1971.

16   (Top) Sutkus addressing officers at the Lithuanian Military Academy on sniper operations and tactics. (Bottom) A reunion at Dortmund station in 1990 with former German Red Cross nurse Erika Regli-Lenz, after forty-five years apart.

17   (Top) Lithuania, 1996: Bruno Sutkus addresses young soldiers of the Lithuanian Army on his skills as a sniper. (Bottom) Sutkus's front-line experiences were scrutinised after Lithuanian independence was obtained. Here he is seen with Lieutenant-Colonel Arvydas Polins and staff of the Lithuanian Army training centre. Lithuanian officers read through his Wehrmacht papers with astonishment.

18 (Top) *Karo meistras* – Master in War – is the title of this long report about Sutkus appearing in the *Lithuanian Echo* of 6 May 1995. (Bottom) In 1995 the Parliamentary Secretary of State and Bundestag Deputy Gertrud Dempwolf visited Sutkus in Vilna, Lithuania in connection with his plea for permission to emigrate to Germany, *Lithuanian Echo*, 7 October 1995.

# RESPUBLIKA

Septintieji leidimo metai    Nr. 284 (1694)    © Lietuvos dienraštis    1995 m. gruodžio 4 d., pirmadienis    Kaina 1.90 Lt

*prenumeratoriams tik 0.96 Lt*

Gražina AŠEMBERGIENĖ

# 209 kartus gyvas

## Susitikimas su vokiečių kariuomenės snaiperiu

### Bruno monologas

"Vis galvoju - nejaugi žmonija dar nepasimokė iš šio baisaus karo. Vokiečiai gal ir būtų laimėję, jeigu būtų žmoniškiau elgęsi. Pirmiausia jiems nereikėjo tyčia žudyti, antra - kaip jūs žiuriai elgėsi su mūsų belaisviais. Bet jei vokiečiai nebūtų puolę 1941 metų birželio 22 dieną - Lietuva galėjo patirti Raudonosios savaitės siaubą - 80 procentų lietuvių turėjo būti sunaikinta arba išvežta į Sibirą. Tai tiesa, nes yra dokumentai. Aš nebuvau nei fašistas, nei komunistas. Jų ideologija mažai kuo skyrėsi".

### Apie jį

- Esu tikras lietuvis, - tvirtina 72 metų Bruno SUTKUS. - Bet taip jau gyvenimas susiklostė...

### Dialogas su Bruno

- Vokiečių kariuomenėje buvote snaiperis. Kaip juo tapote?

- Dar mokymų metu pastebėjo, jog esu taiklus. Vaikystėje turėjau mažo kalibro šautuvą ir šaudydavau žvirblius. Buvau tiesiog jau gerai įsimiklinęs.

### Snaiperis Bruno 1944 metais

### Pirmoji užduotis

- Snaiperių mokyklą baigiau 1943 metų gruodžio mėnesį ir grįžau į dalinį.

1995 metai Vilniuje

Vienintelė Bruno Sutkaus meilė - jo žmona

### Apdovanojimai

- Pagal dokumentus įvykdžius 209 užduotis, - pasakoja Bruno Sutkus, - bet buvo daugiau.

### Panika - mirtis

### Meilė

- Papasakokite, kaip susipažinote su žmona.

Fiurerio vardu jefreitoriui B. Sutkui suteikiamas II laipsnio geležinis kryžius

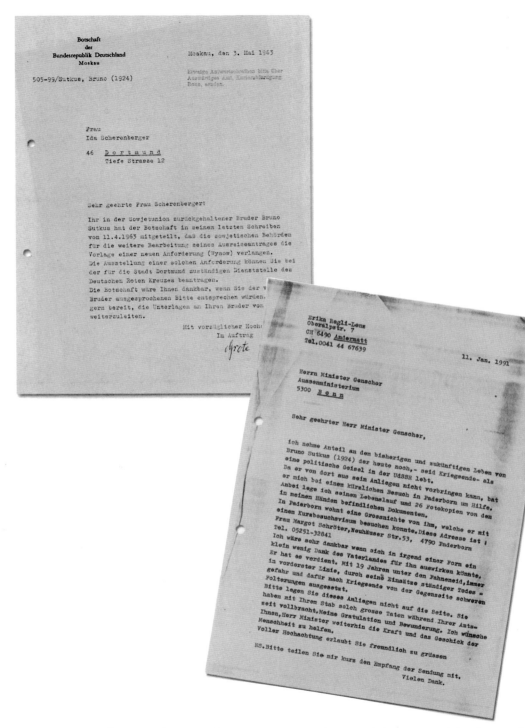

20 (Top) The efforts to obtain Sutkus's papers were long and drawn out. This letter of 3 May 1963 came from the West German Embassy, Moscow. (Bottom) Former German Red Cross Nurse Erika Lenz (now Regli-Lenz) wrote on 11 January 1991 requesting help for Sutkus from the German Foreign Minister Genscher.

# IM NAMEN DES FÜHRERS

### VERLEIHE ICH
### DEM

Gefreiten
Bruno Sutkus
Stab II./Grenadier-Regiment 196

DAS

# EISERNE KREUZ
# 2. KLASSE

Im Felde     den 6.7.     19⁴⁴

(DIENSTSIEGEL)

Generalmajor u. Div.-Kdr.
(DIENSTGRAD UND DIENSTSTELLUNG)

21   Iron Cross 2. Class award certificate, dated 6 July 1944 for Sutkus signed by Generalmajor Paul Scheuerpflug, his divisional commander.

Div.Gef.Std.,den 7.Juli 1944.

An den

Gefreiten Bruno S u t k u s ,

Stab II./Grenadier-Regiment 196.
----------------------------------------

Für Ihre vorbildlichen und hervorragenden

Leistungen als Scharfschütze spreche ich Ihnen

meine ganz besondere Anerkennung

aus.

Generalmajor

22   68. Infantry Division GOC Generalmajor Scheuerpflug letter of 7 July 1944 to Sutkus, expressing his 'very special recognition' of the sniper's 'exemplary and outstanding achievements'.

Abschrift

des Fernschreibens des Oberbefehlshabers der Armeegruppe Heinrici
vom 5.9.44

An
68. Inf.-Division

An Gren. S u t k u s , Stab II./G.R. 196.


Für den 51. Abschuss als Scharfschütze spreche ich dem

Grenadier S u t k u s

meine volle Anerkennung aus.

Ich bewillige einen Sonderurlaub von 14 Tagen.


Der Oberbefehlshaber der Armeegruppe

H e i n r i c i

Generaloberst.

-.-.-.-.-.-.-.-.-.-.-.-.-.-.-

Für die Richtigkeit
der Abschrift:

Major u.Div.-Adj.

3   Authenticated copy of telex, dated 5 September 1944, from Armeegruppe
Heinrici, signed by C-in-C Generaloberst Heinrici, congratulating Sutkus on his fifty-
first success and awarding him fourteen days' special leave.

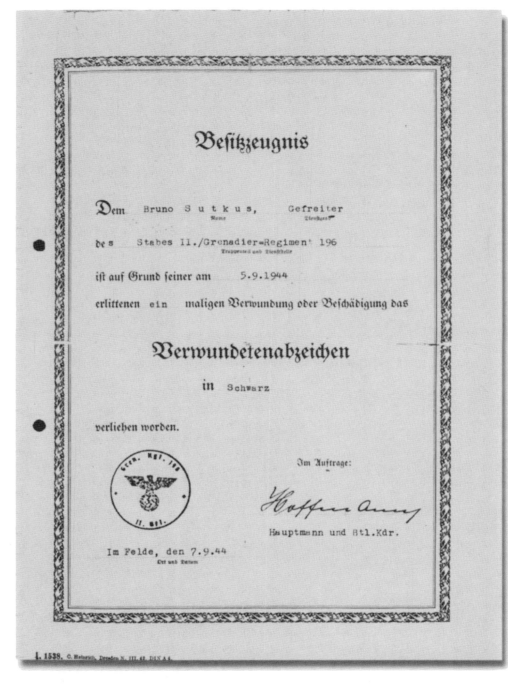

# Besitzeugnis

Dem   Bruno  S u t k u s ,      Gefreiter
           Name                        Dienstgrad

des     Stabes II./Grenadier=Regiment 196
             Truppenteil und Dienststelle

ist auf Grund seiner am     5.9.1944

erlittenen  ein   maligen Verwundung oder Beschädigung das

# Verwundetenabzeichen

in  Schwarz

verliehen worden.

Im Auftrage:

Hauptmann und Btl.Kdr.

Im Felde, den 7.9.44
        Ort und Datum

J. 1538.  C. Heinrich, Dresden N. III. 42. DIN A4.

24    Black class Wound badge award certificate of 7 September 1944 for Sutkus following his injuries of 5 September 1944. Signed by his CO, Hauptmann Herbert Hoffmann commanding II Battalion/Gren Regt 196.

Für hervorragende Leistungen

als Scharfschütze

dem

Gefr. Bruno Sutkus
5.G.R.196

zum 52. Abschuss

als Anerkennung.

Im Osten, den 19.9.44

Der kommandierende General

5 Sniper award card of 19 September 1944 for Sutkus signed by General der ebirgstruppen Karl von Le Suire Commanding General, XXXXIX Gebirgskorps, 'in cognition of outstanding achievements as a sniper' on the occasion of his fifty-second nfirmed claim.

# IM NAMEN DES FÜHRERS
### VERLEIHE ICH
### DEM

Gefreiten
**Bruno  S u t k u s**
Stab II./Grenadier-Regiment 196

### DAS

# EISERNE KREUZ
# 1. KLASSE

........ Im Felde    . den 16.11. 19 44

(DIENSTSIEGEL)

Generalleutnant u. Div.-Kdr.
(DIENSTGRAD UND DIENSTSTELLUNG)

26  Iron Cross 1. Class award certificate, dated 16 November 1944, for Sutkus, signed by 68. Infantry Division GOC Generalleutnant Paul Scheuerpflug.

7 (Top) Commanding General XXXXVIII Panzer Corps Generalleutnant Maximilian Reichsfreiherr von Edelsheim letter to Sutkus, dated 26 November 1944, on the occasion of his 111th success and enclosing a gift in reward. (Bottom) Preliminary advice of 21 November 1944 to Sutkus from Grenadier Regiment 196 of his award of the highest class of the Sniper Proficiency Badge.

28 Preliminary advice to Sutkus from Grenadier Regiment 196 and Silver class award certificate, dated 29 November 1944, for his award of the Infantry Assault Badge.

29 (Top) Sniper award certificate of 23 November 1944 marking Sutkus's seventy-fifth confirmed claim, signed by 4. Panzer-Armee C-in-C General der Panzertruppe Fritz-Hubert Gräser. (Bottom) On the occasion of Sutkus's 150th confirmed claim the author received a presentation watch from the General.

An den

Gefreiten Bruno  S u t k u s

Stab Gren.Rgt. 196

Mit großer Freude habe ich von Ihrem 207. Abschuß gehört. Ich weiß, welcher Mut, welche Ausdauer und Hingabe neben meisterhaftem Können dazu gehören, um diese hervorragende Leistung zu vollbringen. Sie haben damit dem Gegner empfindliche Verluste zugefügt, Ihren Kameraden aber sind Sie ein leuchtendes Beispiel rücksichtsloser Einsatzbereitschaft.

Ich spreche Ihnen dafür meine besondere Anerkennung aus und übersende Ihnen ein Päckchen zu Ihrer persönlichen Verfügung.

H e i l  H i t l e r !

General der Panzertruppe

30  4. Panzer-Armee C-in-C General der Panzertruppe Fritz-Hubert Gräser letter to Sutkus of 11 January 1945 marking his 207th confirmed claim and enclosing a gift.

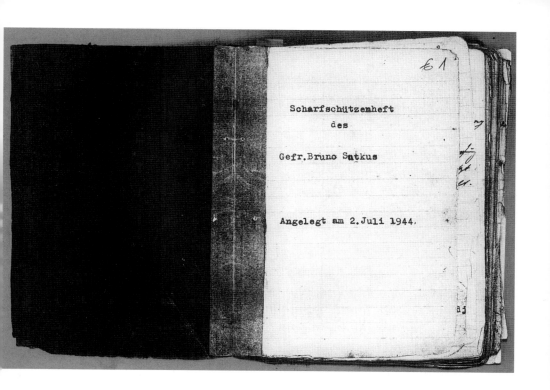

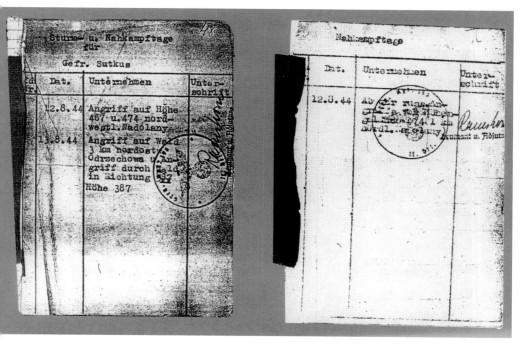

(Above and following pages) Extracts from Sutkus's sniper log (*Scharfschützenheft*)

Abschuss-Nr.: 1.

Datum: 8.5.44

Ort: Slobodka-Lesna
Abschnitt 6/ Gren. Rgt. 196

Vorgang:

1. wurde zur Bekämpfung feindl. Flieger
vor Slobodka-Lesna eingesetzt und am
... feindl. Flieger abgeschossen.
Entfernung: 600 m.
Bezeugt durch: Lt. Walter, Btl. Adj.
– 15.5.44 –

gez. f. d. R!
Neumann
Leutnant u. Btl.Adj.

(Dienstsiegel)
Rgt. 196

---

2

Abschuss-Nr.: 2.

Datum: 9.5.44

Ort: Slobodka-Lesna
Abschnitt 7/ Gren. Rgt. 196

Vorgang:

1. wurde als Bewußtwäge(?) zur
feindl. Fallschirmjäger eingesetzt
... Raum ... Zahl.
... wurde einen Raum ... Zahl.
Entfernung: 300 m.
Bezeugt durch: Lt. Walter, Btl. Adj.
– 15.5.44 –

gez. f. d. R.
Neumann
Leutnant u.Btl.Adj.

(Dienstsiegel)
Rgt. 196

4

Abschuss-Nr.: 5

Datum: 3.7.44

Ort: Gegend Slotoska-Serna nach Clatégorpe-übung.
Abschuß 5./Gren. Rgt. 196

Vorgang:

J. Es wurde in der Stellung der S.Kp. am rechten
Fl. Flügel zur Gefangennahme des Gegners im Wald
an der Polang eingesetzt. Es erlegte als Bewährungs-
Zu- in der Jekewin b. Polang einen Russen.
Br. auf größere Entfernung wegen Baumschutz
mur. Zeitpunkt: 18.00 Uhr.

Entfernung: 600 m.
Beobachtet und Zeuge: Hptm. Küster.

gez. f.d.R.
[signature]
Leutnant u.Btl.Adj.

(Dienstsiegel)
kgl. 196

Abschuss-Nr.: 6

Datum: 3.7.44

Ort: Gegend Slotoska-Serna nach Clatégorpe-übung.
Abschuß 5./Gren. Rgt. 196

Vorgang:

J. wurde in der Stellung der S.Kp. am rechten
Fl. Flügel zur Gefangen- des Gegners im Wald
an der Polang eingesetzt. Es erlegte als Bewährungs-
Zu- in der Jekewin b. Polang einen Russen.
Br. auf größere Entfernung wegen Baumschutz
mur. Zeitpunkt: 18.30 Uhr.

Entfernung: 500 m.
Beobachtet und Zeuge: Hptm. Küster.

gez. f.d.R.
[signature]
Leutnant u.Btl.Adj.

(Dienstsiegel)
kgl. 196

Abschuss-Nr.: 9, 10, 11
Datum: 4. 7. 1944.
Ort: Straße Slobodka-Lesna nach Chlebiczyn-Lesny Abschnitt 7./Gren. Rgt. 196
Vorgang:
S. wurde gegen schlagenden Feind eingesetzt, der in dem Ostrand der Straße den Stellungen der 7. Kp. gegenüber lag. Obwohl durch vorgebaute Blende des Feindes in der Sicht stark behindert, schoß S. 3 anlaufende Russen durch Kopf- oder Brustschuß gefechtsunfähig. Entfernung: 200 m. Zeit: 20.30-21.00
Bezeugt: Gefr. Hepler (1)

Gren. Rgt. 196 (Dienstsiegel) II. Btl.

gez. f.d.R.
[Unterschrift]
Leutnant u. Btl.Adj.

Abschuss-Nr.: 12, 13, 14, 15, 16.
Latum: 5. 7. 1944
Ort: Straße Slobodka-Lesna nach Chlebiczyn-Lesny Abschnitt 7./Gren. Rgt. 196
Vorgang: Zeit: 4.00-6.00 Uhr
Bei der Bekämpfung mit heran schleichender Russen wurde S. zunächst in ein Duell mit sichernden russ. Baumschützen verwickelt (Scharfsch.), den er mit 2 Schüssen vom Baum schoß. Anschließend setzte S. 4 vorgeschobene Russen außer Gefecht, wobei er sich in eine exponierte Stellung 50 m vor dem Graben begab und mehrfach beschossen wurde. Entf.: 200 m.
Bezeugt: Lt. Kaul Stabsgefr.

Gren. Rgt. 196 (Dienstsiegel) II. Btl.

gez. f.d.R.:
[Unterschrift]
Leutnant u. Btl.Adj.

Abschuss-Nr.: 17 u. 18

Datum: 6. 7. 44.

Ort: Luna-Stellung nördl. Magyarenschlucht
Abschnitt 5./Gren. Rgt. 196

Vorgang:

Um 5.00 Uhr arbeitete sich S. selbständig mit 2 Zeugen in das gegenüber der Stellung liegende Waldgelände vor und setzte in der Luna-Stellung 1 russ. Posten durch Kopfschuß außer Gefecht.
Ein 2. Russe, durch den Schuß angelockt, die Stellung überquerend, wurde ebenfalls von S. niedergeschossen.
Entfernung: 100 m.

Bezeugt: Uffz. Hergel, Gefr. Müller.

gez. f.d.R.

(Dienstsiegel)

Ramshorn
Leutnant u. Btl.Adj



Abschuss-Nr.: 19 u. 20

Datum: 6. 7. 44.

Ort: Luna-Stellung nördl. Magyarenschlucht
Abschnitt 5./Gren. Rgt. 196

Vorgang:

1/4 Stunde nach Abschuß von Nr. 18 bemerkte S. einen feindl. Spähtrupp in Stärke von 7 Mann, der sich ihm von links in einer Entfernung von 150 m näherte.
S. schoß den M.G.-Schützen 1 desselben nieder u. arbeitete sich auf die Stellung der 5. Kp. zurück.
Von dort schoß er aus dem sich in Gegend der [illegible] Luna-Stellung vorschiebenden Spähtrupp einen Russen, anscheinend Offizier heraus. Entfernung: 150 m.

Bezeugt: Uffz. Hergel, Gefr. Müller. gez. f.d.R.

(Dienstsiegel)

Ramshorn
Leutnant u. Btl.Adj.

Abschuss-Nr.: 24

Datum: 7.7.1944

Ort: Anna-Shenino nördl. Magyarenulklid(?)
Abschnitt 5./Gren. Rgt. 196

Vorgang:

In den Mandelstrücken wurde S. wiederum in
Abschnitt "Anna-Shenino" zur Feuerauf...
den Schützen in dieser Scheune angezeigt. In
einer Entfernung von 600 m setzte er einen
... Volltreffer, der diese Scheune übergepackt,
ab.

Zeit: 22.00 Uhr.

Bezeugt: O.Gren. Behrend.

(Dienstsiegel)

gez.f.d.R.

[Unterschrift] hm
Leutnant u. Btl.Adj.

Abschuss-Nr.: 25 + 26

Datum: 7.7.1944

Ort: Anna-Shenino nördl. Magyarenulklid(?)
Abschnitt 5./Gren. Rgt. 196

Vorgang:

Etwa 9 Russen, die durch den Hohlweg Nr.21
S. als Sammelplatz erkannt hatten, auffanden
auf der M.G. u. M.Pi. Stellungen. Trotzdem steht S. auf
dem Baum u. setzt den M.Pi.Schützen 2 ohne Hüft...
... wieder. Seinen weiteren Schützen setzt er von
einem Baum aus, er ... u. S. um fällt. Seine
Kampfgebiet hat, ab. Entfernung: 350 m
Bezeugt: Obstl. Behrend.    Zeit: 20.05 Uhr.

gez. f.d.R.

Ramson
Leutnant u. Btl.Adj.    Dienstsiegel

Abschuss-Nr.: 42/43

Datum: 17.7.1944

Ort: Magyarenschlucht

Abschnitt 5./G.R. 196

Vorgang:

S. arbeitete sich etwa 250 m vor die H.K.L. auf eine Höhe, von welcher er das Gelände besser übersehen konnte. Er konnte von dieser Stelle aus 2 russ. V.B., die in einer Entfernung von 300 m auf Bäumen saßen, abschießen.

Zeuge: Gren. Baumann.

Gren. Rgt. 196 · II. Btl.

(Dienstsiegel)

gez. f.d.R.

Leutnant u. Btl.Adj.

---



Abschuss-Nr.: 44, 45, 46 u. 47

Datum: 26.7.1944 (16.15 Uhr)

Ort: Höhe 324 an Straße Skwirska-Gielowice

Abschnitt 5./Gren. Rgt. 196

Vorgang: Als Melder zum Btl.Kdr. eingesetzt, bekam S. aus einer Entfernung von ca. 700 m Inf. Feuer von einem russ. Stoßtrupp unter Führung von 2 Offiziere. Beide Offiziere schoß S. kurz hintereinander nieder. Die dadurch entstehende Verwirrung unter den Russen ausnutzend, wechselte S. seine Feuerstellung und schoß 2 M.G.-Schützen nieder. Entfernung: 200 m

Zeuge: Gefr. Schüppenthau

Gren. Rgt. 196 · II. Btl.

(Dienstsiegel)

gez. f.d.R.

Leutnant u. Btl.Adj.

Abschuss-Nr.: 48

Datum: 12.8.44   Zeit: 17.xx

Ort: Höhe 467, 2 km ostw. Odzechowa

Vorgang: Bei der Ausführung eines
Befehls, von Stehenden Dörnern einen
gelaxene Pferde einzufangen, als
S. einem Bauern in einer Entfernung
von 100 m durch Brustschuß nieder.

Zeuge: Gfr. Binder

gez. f.d.R.

Pellerha
Leutnant u.Btl.Adj.

(Dienstsiegel)

---

Abschuss-Nr.: 49

Datum: 12.8.44

Ort: Höhe 467, 2 km ostw. Odzechowa

Vorgang: Bei der Erfüllung eines Auf-
trages aufgegen zog S. in den Zigen,
füh eine Rauen wieder, ob deren
auf die Zeugen aufgelegt hatte, Auf 10 m.
Vor einem Rebenhäufen brachte die Zukünftige
aufgelösten unter 4 Schuten 1 einen Zugen
Schutzen wird. Zeit: 18.75

freig: Gfr. Laubstal

gez. F.d.R.

Leutnant u.Btl.Adj.

(Dienstsiegel)

Abschuss—Nr.: 99.92

Datum: 15.11.44
Ort: Karmelice

Vorgang: _[handschriftlich, unleserlich]_

Entfernung: 500 m    Zeit 4.30 h
Zeuge: Gefr. Keller

gez.f.d.R.

(Dienstsiegel)        Leutnant u.Btl.Adj.

---

Abschuss—Nr.: 99

Datum: 15.11.44
Ort: Karmelice

Vorgang: _[handschriftlich, unleserlich]_

Zeuge: Gefr. Keller

Ru 88 - 109

gez. f.d.R.

(Dienstsiegel)        Leutnant u. BtlAdj.

Abschuss-Nr.: 99

Datum: 15.11.44

Ort:

Vorgang: *[handschriftlicher Text, unleserlich]*

gez.f.d.R.

(Dienstsiegel) gez. Schäfer

Leutnant u. Btl.Adjt.

---

Abschuss-Nr.: 94.-98

Datum: 15.11.44

Ort: Jagdweise

Vorgang: *[handschriftlicher Text, unleserlich]*

gez.f.d.R.

(Dienstsiegel)

Leutnant u.Btl.Adj.

Geschäfts-Nr.: 112 - 113

Datum: 22.11.44

Ort:

Gegenstand:

---

Geschäfts-Nr.: 110/111

Datum: 19.11.44

Ort: bei Brückenbau

Gegenstand:

Bericht Nr.: 115.116
Datum: 28.11.44
Ort: Kazmeliec

Vorgang: ...

gez. ...
Leutnant u. Kp. Chef.

---

Bericht Nr.: 114
Datum: 28.11.44
Ort: bei Kazmeliec

Vorgang: ...

Leutnant u. Kp. Chef.

8

---

Abschnitts-Nr. 150 - 151

Datum: 17.12.44

Ort: b. Hagenau

Vorgang: Nach dem erzielten Abschuss 1½
beobachtete S. zwei in... Schütze...
148-149 beobachtete S. zwei in... Schütze
...mit Beobachter in Stellung ging.
S. ...... den Beobachter durch Kopf-
schuss auf 250 m ab. In dem ... fort-
... Feuer mit dem ... Scharfschützen ge-
nannten Stelle mit dem ... Scharfschützen ge-
Nun ... Sch. S. ... diesen durch Kopf-
schuss ... ...

Zeuge: Sgt. Diebold – 5.Kp.

Leutnant u. Batl.Adjutant

---

Abschnitts-Nr. 152

Datum: 17.12.44

Ort: Fastzgehör

Vorgang: Auf dem Wege von Kp. Gef.St. der
7.Kp. ... Stellung ... S. auf ... um Entfernung
von 400 m zwei ... Melder, ... ...
einen ... Schützen ... in die Stellung ging
ohne Deckung zu nehmen. Diese ... ....
S. durch Brustschuss ab.

Zeuge: Ogfr. Hauptvogel – 7.Kp.

Leutnant u. Batl.Adjutant

Abschuss-Nr. 173

Datum: 30.12.44

Ort: Jachgebiet.

Vorgang: In den Vormittagsstunden er-
greift S. einen Russen, der von Flk. Horvat
aus, den Weg zu den Bunkern einschlug.
Als er eine freie Fläche im Obstgarten
überschritt erhob S. den Russen den Russen
auf eine Entfernung von 300 m durch
Pistolenschuss ab.

Zeuge: Obgfr. Klaffron   -   5. Kp.

Leutnant u. Flk. Adjutant.

---

Abschuss-Nr. 172

Datum: 30.12.44

Ort: Jachgebiet.

Vorgang: Abends gegen 8.00 Uhr früh beschoss S. in dichter Nähe rechts vom Gehöft
in sicherer Sicht einen russ. Postenstein, welcher
von dort aus das Gehöft bestr. Feuer gab
konnte drückte. Diesen Russen erhob S. auf
eine Entfernung von 400 m durch Pistolenschuss
ab.

Zeuge: O.Grm. Arnold   -   5. Kmpe.

Leutnant b. Flk. Adjutant.

Abschuss Nr.: 175.

Datum: 30.12.44

Ort: Jasligehie.

Vorgang: Nach dem Stielschuss mit dem
..., Scharfschützen eröffnet 1/mo. M.P. - und
1/mo. MG. Schütze auf S. das Feuer. S. war
gezwungen in Deckung zu bleiben. Als ein
..., (50 m) ...,
eigenes MG. eingestellt, wurde hinter das Feuer
auf die Russen eröffnet, wurden diese abge-
bekzt und hierbei gelang es dem S. den poln.
M.P. Schützen bei einem Stellungswechsel ohne
Beobachtung abzuwimdern. Schussstellung
350 m.

Entfernung: Obgfr. Pfeffer.                    5. Kp.

Leutnant u. Jdl. Kompietant.

---

Abschuss Nr. 174.

Datum: 30.12.44

Ort: Jasligehie.

Vorgang: Nach Beziehung des PB. Abschnitts ver-
mochte der Sigma ohne Bewegung eine Scharfschützen,
eines M.P. - und eines MG. Schützen eines Tr. S. aus-
zumachen. S. erblickte plötzlich den Scharfschützen
des feld. Scharfschützen, sprang in Deckung und wehrte
während des Beginns in die Grabenwand.
Klirrt ... viel S. und schoss den poln.
Scharfschützen auf 300 m ab. Bei ... einen
Korporal ausgelöste schoss des mo. Scharfschützen
Tage mitt zur ...

Zeuge: Obgfr. Pfeffer.                   5. Kp.

Leutnant u. Jdl. Kompietant.

Abschrift-Nr. 176.

Datum: 30.12.44

Ort: Jastzebie.

Vorgang: Nach dem vorhergegangenen Alarm ...
... die Russen das Feuer ...
S. erkannte das Mündungsfeuer und kam in ...
... die Granate über S. hinweg in ...
... die Grabenwand ... Sfz. 9. Infant ...
... Einzelschuss ... 50 m ...
... S. ... aus ... über den ...
... Erd Boden
... in Richtung des Infant ...
Die Schussweite beträgt S. ... einem ...
... auf 338 m ... ab.

Zeuge: Sfz. 9. Infant.
5. Kp.

Leutnant u. Flt. Adjutant

---

Abschrift-Nr. 177.

Datum: 30.12.44

Ort: Jastzebie

Vorgang: Auf dem ... Flt. ... einer ...
S. ... durch Uffz. Brüller gesehen. Beim ...
... in Kopf ...
... S. ...
... Pinzeau, ... auf die Deckung ...
... und lag ... auf die Deckung.
Nach einem 2. Schuss ... die Russ Bewegung ...
... auf die Deckung ... Schussentfernung
600 m.

Zeuge: Uffz. Brüller
5. Kp.

Leutnant u. Flt. Adjutant

Abschuß - Nr. 178

Datum: 3.1.45

Ort: Jaszgdwin.

Hergang: Um 9.00 betrachtete S. einen
Russen, der vom Bunker weg, in ein Haus
lief. Als der Russe kurze Zeit darauf das
Haus wieder verlassen wollte schoß Sothero
denselben auf Entfernung von 600 m in
die Haustür durch Brustschuß ab.

Zeuge: Gefr. Bebringer    - 7 Uhr.

Leutnant u. Kp.-Führer.

[Stamp: GREN. REG. 190]

---

Abschuß - Nr. 179

Datum: 3.1.45

Ort: Jaszgdwin.

Hergang: Gegen 15.30 bargen die Russen
Russen, die vom Bunker weg...
... Ablösungen die Stellungen. Als 1 Russe
sich mit halber Körperhöhe über einen
MG. Stellung zeigte, wurde dieser von
S. durch Brustschuß abgeschossen.
Schußentfernung: 600 m.

Zeuge: Gefr. Bräuer    - 7.45.

Leutnant u. Kp.-Führer.

[Stamp: GREN. REG. 190]

Abschrift - Nr. 207.

Datum: 7.1.45

Ort: Jachybnie.

Vorgang: Gegen 15.30 Uhr sah S. einen Zug, der vor der Stellungen ihren Posten ging. Er wurde von S. auf 400 m abge-schossen.

Zeuge: Schf. Hardt – Zug.

Leutnant u. Btl. Adjutant.


Abschrift - Nr. 200.

Datum: 7.1.45

Ort: Jachybnie.

Vorgang: Nach dem vorausgegangenen Beschießen wurde S. von einem ... Unterständen ... Feuer genommen. S. erhielt einen Posten nach rechts mit dem Gegner zu bekämpfen. Seine Posten hob eine Klappe über dem Erdverband auf, wobei der Russ feuert. Da der ... Klappschütze einen Schutzschild hatte, kann er nach rechts. Hierbei wurde er von ... fort ... 300 m abgeschossen.

Zeuge: Obgfr. Scheel – Zug.

Leutnant u. Btl. Adjutant.

# ~ PART TWO~

# 1

## *The End of the War: Escaping the Firing Squad*

The Second World War ended on 8 May 1945. The victors occupied our German homeland. I was under medical care at Burgstädt until 25 May 1945, when the Americans allowed me to be discharged to the care of my parents. I knew where Red Cross nurse Erika lived, and I travelled to Nastätten near Wiesbaden, staying there until July 1945. There was no longer any talk of marriage: Erika said that if Germany had won the war all would have been different, but as it was my mother needed me more. She advised me to speak to an American colonel in Wiesbaden who had a proposal for me. This turned out to be an opening for an armed security officer working at a gold and diamond mine in the Congo. The contract was for several years. The snag was that beforehand the colonel expected me to accompany his military unit to the Far East where I would probably be expected to snipe freelance. I told him I was not for sale. When he argued that we had wanted 'to conquer the world', I pointed out that the United States had helped the Russians slaughter us in our efforts to save Europe from the Red menace. The Americans had betrayed us, costing millions of lives. The United States was interested only in the financial benefits war brought: they had helped the Red lice and now they would have to deal with them. The colonel advised me that if I would not sign his contract I should seek work in Wiesbaden – if I returned to my mother in Leipzig the Russians would arrest me for sure. When I retorted that all I had been was a simple soldier at the front, he said I should not be so naive: they would either put me on trial for my life or I might get lucky and be sent to a forced-labour camp in Siberia.

---

I returned to my parents at Stöbnich near Leipzig. They could not return to East Prussia, where the Russians were in occupation. My mother was caring for the three small orphaned daughters of a childhood friend. It was my hope to bring them all out of the Russian zone of occupation, but on the second night back I was arrested by the Russians. German communists had denounced me to the Soviets as a former Wehrmacht sniper. The Russians were very sensitive about snipers and according to their standing orders enemy snipers were not to be treated as prisoners of war but shot immediately on capture.

My mother had learnt some Russian in the school at Leketschai where she taught, and she approached the competent SMERSH (Soviet counter-intelligence) lieutenant-colonel for my release, since I was her only son. This, together with a bribe of French cognac (given to me by General Gräser) and my grandfather's gold signet ring, impressed him. I bitterly regret the loss of the ring. It bore the coat of arms of my aristocratic grandfather – a count – whose illegitimate and unwanted son was my father. I had no documents attesting to my father's ancestry.

It will be remembered that in 1940, when I was sixteen, I had been granted a Foreigner's Identity Card by the Reich authorities that allowed me to reside at Schlossberg as a stateless person. Although I was subsequently naturalised as German, I had retained the card, which now came in very useful. The bribed SMERSH officer ordered the occupation police to validate the card to the present, thus making me stateless again, and I was issued with a forged certificate stating that throughout the war I had worked as a farm labourer. However the lieutenant-colonel advised my mother that I should make myself scarce as soon as possible.

My parents and I now entered one of the emigration camps set up in Eastern Germany by the Soviets. We moved from one camp to another and were interrogated by the NKVD, the Soviet secret police. Each time my Foreigner's Identity Card and the certificate showing I had never served as a German soldier kept me safe. Eventually a big round-up of young men took place. In August 1945 we were loaded aboard railway cattle trucks at Altenburg/ Saxony, to arrive a month later at Brest-Litovsk. Once across the Soviet frontier, all men who had not served previously in the Soviet Army were detained for military service in the Soviet Union. Here all the tears and pleading of my mother would cut no ice. I was conscripted into the Red Army!

Crammed into a train filled with recruits, heading slowly for Russia, I stood in the doorway near the armed guard. As we pulled away from the station, another train was arriving at Brest-Litovsk from the east. I jumped out into the path of the other locomotive. The guard was surprised and had no time to react before I rolled to the far side of the other train for cover.

I returned to Leipzig. My mother was with the three orphaned Steppat children. She was ill and being attended by a nurse. A Russian patrol scoured the neighbourhood looking for me. I put on the nurse's coat, wound a bandage round my head and sat with the Steppat children. The Russians overlooked me. Each night a goods train came through Leipzig bound for Vilnius, the capital of Lithuania. We bribed the locomotive driver to smuggle us aboard because it required the authority of the Soviets to cross the frontier. Once in Lithuania, my aunt at Shetiya gave us shelter. I probably owe my life to her husband, a local government officer. He forged me a birth certificate showing my birthplace as Patashei, and that my father was also Lithuanian.

Things were still on a war footing in Lithuania. We settled later in Pashegshdrai, my mother's home town, where relations helped us out. My mother was forced to beg in the streets to help feed the three orphaned girls; I did not earn enough to feed a whole family. That winter of 1945 German women and children came to Lithuania from the devastated villages of East Prussia. They begged for food, and were close to starvation. The Lithuanians helped to alleviate their distress. They were the flotsam of war, the survivors of the brutal expulsion of the Germans from East Prussia. Soon I found work on the Povelaitis farm, which was run by the wife. The husband had supported the Lithuanian resistance movement against the Russians, as a result of which he had been taken away by the Russians.

In December 1945 I headed for East Prussia. Everywhere I found the most terrible devastation. I crossed the Scheschuppe, which had not yet frozen over. The border was heavily guarded. This was often fatal for homecoming German soldiers who had escaped from Soviet captivity. As the Soviets maintained a state of war in Lithuania until 1953, Germans on the run were arrested and shot when caught. At Fichtenhöhe, my home village, I found Arno

Braemer's farmstead. All the buildings – stalls, the silo and stables, even our house – still stood, or at least the half that had not caved in, but inside all was totally destroyed. The rest of the village was abandoned and reduced to ruins.

Cautiously I made my way to the neighbouring village of Herbstfelde – it was the same story, with wild and unruly dogs barking at me. I headed for Willuhnen, hoping to find a sign of life. From the moor near the edge of the woods I could see that the road was mined. Cautiously I went into a few ruined farmsteads, peering into the dwelling houses. Everything was devastated: missing window frames, furniture hacked to pieces. Despite the mines I had to pass through the woodland. The depressions in the soil showed me where the mines had been laid. If I trod on one here I could expect no help. Dusk was falling. In the distance I saw smoke rising from a farmhouse. A horse and cart had just driven off with some Russian soldiers. I dared not go near until I saw a woman emerge to fetch water from a stream. As I approached she dropped her bucket in surprise. It was an emotional reunion. She knew me from the occasions when I had visited my sister Ida in the village. She told me that the Russians had just left, they had been looking for weapons and German soldiers returning home.

I accompanied her home. Inside was another woman whose husband lay on a bed. He had lost both feet in the fighting on the Eastern Front. Near him his twelve-year-old daughter lay dying. Her sexual organs had been deliberately injured after she was brutally raped by Soviet soldiers, who had forced the parents to watch. The child's sexual organs were filled with blood and suppurating. The Russians had battered the father's head with their rifle butts when he protested. The mother had offered herself to spare the daughter, but the Russians had merely laughed and eight of them did what they wanted sexually with the child.

The Pägers family lived eight kilometres from Willuhnen, near the lake. They recounted many similar events and wept at the appalling atrocities committed by the Russians. An endless Red blight swept the land. I learnt from them that in March 1945 a group of German prisoners of war were shot on the Willuhnen Lake. Then the Russians blew up the ice to destroy the evidence. I spent the night with the Pägers. They warned me not to go to Willuhnen.

Next day on the Schlossberg–Neustadt road towards Lithuania I watched large Soviet troop movements. I simply had to get to Willuhnen to hide out before attempting my return to Fichtenhöhe. Where the Schlossberg Church had been the Russians had erected a monument to their war dead. Of the German military cemetery, which had once been opposite, there was no trace. The grounds had run to weed, the grave markers gone. By now I had naturally abandoned any idea of making a new life for my family in the Schlossberg district. The area was almost totally depopulated and the traces of German life wiped away. All that remained was senseless destruction from Eydkuhnen to Tilsit. Schlossberg was at the heart of a dead zone. The Scheschuppe had not yet frozen over and I swam the ice-cold water to the other side. I returned to my parents at Pashegshdrai. We gave up our dream of beginning a new life in our former homeland, East Prussia – it was impossible.

On 15 December 1945 the NKVD came. They were pressganging young men for the Soviet military induction office at Grishkabudes. I was caught up in it. A medical found me fit for active duty, and I was detained, kept locked up at night in a lorry and finally transported under heavy guard with others to a Soviet artillery unit at Gumbinnen in East Prussia. We were kitted out in old, stinking Soviet uniforms. The heavy guard was not relaxed. I was worried that I might speak German in my sleep and so betray myself. I surveyed the terrain closely since I intended to bolt. We were given a change of uniform in order to swear the Red Army oath. Next day our unit was shipping out to the far east of the USSR. The time had come for action.

That night I crept stealthily from my tent. The guard stood freezing on the corner. I ran – he saw me and fired at my back. The bullet hit me, close to my spinal column. Now I ran for my life. The alarm had been sounded. I kept on going, blood seeping from the wound. I had no first-aid dressings. My first problem was to get through the former front line with its uncleared minefields. This forced me to wait for morning, by which time I had lost a lot of blood and was weak. By day I had to hide up to avoid being spotted by Russian soldiers. I found a half-ruined house with no windows, devastated inside. I settled in a dark corner of the cellar to rest. In the opposite corner were the remains of a woman. She had been shot through the head, legs spread wide, clothing torn, raped by the Russians. A kindly bullet to her brain had ended her torment. When night fell I left.

On the third day I reached the Scheschuppe River. Ice floes drifted by. I undressed and waded through the bitterly cold water. My objective was the village of Senlakai, eight kilometres down from Fichtenhöhe, where my aunt had lived and I was known. At a farmstead I lost consciousness after being taken in. Justinus Baukus removed the bullet from my spine and sealed the wound with a white-hot iron. After three weeks' nursing I was fit enough to return to my parents at Pashegshdrai. They warned me that I was liable to be arrested as a deserter. I was now left with no option but to remain with the Lithuanian resistance. They took me in, hid me and healed me.

# 2

## *Helping the Lithuanian Resistance*

*Lithuania had been independent since the First World War. In June 1940 the Soviet Union occupied and annexed Lithuania under the Molotov–Ribbentrop Pact. After the Wehrmacht drove out the Russians in the summer of 1941, groups of Lithuanian men served in various defence units in collaboration with the Germans. These units fought Soviet and Polish partisans. The Soviet Union regained control in late 1944. From then until 1952, approximately 100,000 Lithuanians participated in partisan activities against the Soviet occupiers. More than 20,000 freedom fighters were killed and many more deported to Siberia. The Soviets employed the most cruel methods of torture and behaved bestially. Lithuanian historians view this period as a war of independence against the Soviet Union. During the period of occupation between 1940 and 1944, the Soviets murdered or exiled up to 300,000 of the population, while the Nazis accounted for the removal of most of the rest, including 91 per cent of the Lithuanian pre-war Jewish population.*

~

All my documents had been confiscated by the Russians. Passing through Leketschai I was stopped by the NKVD. They thought I looked suspicious and demanded my identity card. Since I could not produce it I was arrested as a 'bandit' and 'Lithuanian terrorist'. They wanted to know where my bunker was and I was beaten. Afterwards my hands were bound behind my back with wire and at Grishkabudes jail I was tortured. The NKVD-instructed judge wanted me to admit to being a German soldier. I was also told to reveal the hideouts of the Lithuanians terrorists and reveal where my other associates were to be found. I spent three weeks in that jail. It was a dreadful place. Each person was allowed two square feet of space. There was no room to sit or lie down. One had to remain standing the whole time, and sleep standing. Often during this time I cursed my fate and regretted not having fallen for Germany at the front. A cousin helped me. For a bribe of smoked ham, sausage and vodka, KGB Captain Shelebinas intervened on my behalf just before my trial. The prosecutor was asking for the death sentence by shooting for desertion. My Foreigner's Identity Card from Schlossberg in his possession proved that I was not Lithuanian because I was born in Germany, and as a stateless person I did not have Soviet nationality and so could not be found guilty of treason and desertion under Section 58 of their criminal code. I was released and given a document bestowing upon me the right to live in Shakai. Once again I had narrowly escaped death.

My cousin Pyus obtained work for me on the former farm of the Povelaitis family. The husband had been arrested for collaboration with the resistance. His wife Antoniena – Toni – was a teacher in the school at Leketschai. The family had been dispossessed in 1944 when the Russians returned to Lithuania. For the year from 25 March 1946 I was the fourth farm manager before the business was transferred to the cooperative. My predecessors had all been assassinated by the resistance.

My cousin Antone arrived there at Christmas 1946. Her husband and brother were both involved with the resistance. She supplied the resistance with bread, did their laundry and asked me to provide them with cereals. What they most sorely lacked was medicines, particularly penicillin. I discovered later that Toni often travelled to Kauen, where she had a good relationship with the professor at the hospital there. He gave her penicillin and dressings, which she passed to me or other resistance fighters. In the autumn during the threshing I managed to set aside three sacks of grain, despite the watchful eyes of the commission, and forwarded them to Antone. This was not the last I heard of these three sacks.

On 16 February 1947 a number of partisan bunkers in the Kurakaimas forest were betrayed. Soviet troops surrounded the bunkers and called on the occupants to surrender. Rather than go through the usual Soviet torture processes they shot themselves.

The corpses were desecrated sexually by the Russians and put on public display in the police-station courtyard. Amongst them was the mutilated body of the young schoolteacher Grashina Matulaite and her fiancé. The Russians ruled Lithuania with murder, pillage and terror, and plundered the lifeblood of the people: a life had no value. At Yalta in 1943, Roosevelt, Stalin and Churchill gifted the Baltic states of Lithuania, Estonia and Latvia to the Soviet Union. The people under the yoke cursed Stalin, but the governments of the United States and Britain loved him and supported him.

In February 1946 Lithuania had a general election. All candidates had to be communist. The people boycotted the election and therefore the KGB and NKVD filled in the ballot papers on their behalf. They were 'voting for the people', they said, and this was the democratic manner in which the election was decided. On May Day 1947 everybody had to demonstrate his or her loyalty to Stalin, the government and the Communist Party. There was to be a long parade. I was obliged to carry a banner bearing the slogan 'Stalin Our Great Teacher' and 'Dear Communist Party'. I held one pole and Jurgelis the other. Jurgelis was a miller and on this day turned up the worse for drink. The forestry workers' group preceded us, proudly hoisting Stalin's portrait. There was a platform on which the Communist Party bosses and officers of the NKVD and KGB were standing, and before this platform was a large puddle. Approaching the platform Jurgelis stumbled and fell. Our banner with its slogans and portrait of Stalin fell into the puddle. Jurgelis and I were arrested at once, but the village of Leketschai could not function long without a miller and so we were released two days later.

After the parade, Toni Povelaitis (my future wife) was ordered to provide a concert with her higher-level students. Laudatory poems and songs were required. The school director read and confirmed the proposed programme, which unfortunately involved no mention of either Stalin or the Communist Party, and the poems also spoke of an enslaved people in prisons and fighting for their freedom no matter how long it took. The party bosses did not like the look of this programme, and Toni was arrested. Thanks to the intervention of the school director there was no political trial, but on 25 March 1949 Toni suffered banishment to Siberia with her whole family as a result of it. She was allowed to continue as secretary of the middle school until her deportation, but on a much reduced salary.

Toni told me her story. She was a schoolteacher, her husband a senior forester. They had owned a rich farm with fine new buildings. At the end of July 1944 there was fierce fighting for Vilnius. The German defenders were surrounded, and not many managed to get out. A large number of their wounded were housed in the St Peter and Paul Church. The Russians dug a large mass grave and threw the 668 German wounded from the windows of the church into the grave and buried them alive. There are witnesses still alive who recall this NKVD atrocity. Countless murdered German troops are entombed in Vingis Park, and today their bones rest below a children's playground.

At the end of August 1944, near the Povelaitis farm, a Soviet military recruitment office was set up, run by a Captain, Matestovich, a drinker never slow to accept a bribe. The Russians used the pressgang system to find recruits for Matestovich. The operations were conducted at night, men and youths being kidnapped at gunpoint from their beds for military service. If the mothers and wives could afford it, bribes were brought by the Povelaitis family to Matestovich. Smoked ham, sausage and other commodities would purchase a document from Matestovich certifying unfitness for Soviet military service, which meant release.

In the autumn of 1944 the borders of East Prussia became the front line. From all over Lithuania, young men were sent to the front to fight the Germans after three days' training. This meant certain death. Only a warped Bolshevik mind could have dreamt up such a tactic. At the front, special units of NKVD commissars stood at the recruits' backs, pistols drawn, to prevent these press-ganged foreigners running for it. Many of them were shot down from behind while refusing to advance on the German lines. Many young men in Lithuania, who were not Russian, and certainly not citizens of the Soviet Union, were not prepared to be used as cannon fodder at the front for the interests of this alien state – they fled to the forests to join resistance groups fighting against the Soviet occupiers.

In the epoch of Lithuanian independence from 1941 to 1944, Toni's husband Antanas Povelaitis worked with a neighbouring forester, the communist Matulonis. They were constantly at odds on political matters. When the Russians regained control in 1944, Matulonis was appointed minister and commissar for forestry. Antanas was arrested by the Sovets on Matulonis's say-so and the contents of his home confiscated. At a hearing he received ten years' forced labour and was banished to Siberia for life. Antoniena was allowed to remain on the farm, provided she lived in the hen-house. Glikas, a collaborator and leader of the NKVD agents at Shakai, came to inform her that she was dispossessed of everything, 'including the spoon you eat with'.

In the torture chambers of the NKVD the partisan Animashukas from Genshai was turned by the NKVD into their agent. At the end of February 1947 he fingered me and I was arrested. He alleged that I was a German war criminal who had supplied three sacks of grain to the resistance. He also alleged truthfully that I had possessed a sub machine gun and a Walther pistol. My cousin Antone and her husband were also arrested and tortured but did not give me away. The Soviets wanted to know all about the three sacks of grain and where I got the penicillin from that I gave to the resistance. They also wanted the weapons.

My hands were bound and the Russian sadist and torture expert Lieutenant Kiselov arrived to practise his art. Since I did not cry out and only groaned at the pain the Russians became annoyed, and I was thrown into a room and left to reconsider. Next evening an escaped German soldier was brought in. Since the state of war in Lithuania remained in force, all Germans found abroad without a Soviet release document from the PoW authorities were shot. The German soldier suffered this fate next morning. Afterwards I was shown his body. They asked me for the last time if I was going to talk – if not I would be shot. I refused to talk, and said they should go ahead and do what they had in mind. They wanted to blindfold me. I waved this away and stormed, 'Get it over with.' The sadist Kiselov placed a matchbox on my head and fired at it. He hit the matchbox and then reholstered his weapon saying that a bullet was too good for me – a Fascist dog like me should go to a place where I would rot to death.

Antoniena agreed with my mother to bribe KGB Captain Shulebin for my release. Crystal glasses, vodka, smoked hams and clothing were offered to the Russian officer via an interpreter. The following morning I was discharged for lack of evidence regarding the supply of provisions to the partisans. My mother hardly recognised me. My face was black and blue and swollen from the beatings. My fingernails had all been torn out. My back was covered in weals and the flesh had burst open in various places.

A priest let me know that the relevant authorities were actively seeking a replacement for me as manager of the Povelaitis farm, but nobody would do it because everyone knew my situation with Toni. In the spring of 1948 I was recognised by the Soviet stooge Maskevichus Komsorg, who knew that I had been a German sniper. I denied this in the presence of KGB Chairman Shulebenas, but now they were suspicious. Was I German or Lithuanian? Perhaps I wanted to return to my German Fatherland, in which case might they allow me to travel? The NKVD people laughed. They knew which Fatherland I would be sent to. The big mass graves of murdered German prisoners still wait to be found in the Lithuanian forests.

In January 1948 my mother died. After her funeral I sat at the table at home and wept. The three orphan children of Maria Steppat watched me. Relatives adopted them.

I wined and dined the new interrogating judge, Kondrashov. He came along later with an arrest warrant for me. The indictment stated that I was a German officer who had been sent here on a spying mission. He threw the documents in the fire – once again fate had been kind to me. Toni and I again invited Kondrashov and the new chairman, Captain Kruglov, to dine with us. Under the influence of too much alcohol Kruglov advised me to leave Leketschai at the earliest and go to Memel, where nobody knew us.

Toni and I were aware that preparations were in hand to banish her to Siberia and arrest me. The danger was immense. I always felt that they had never really forgotten me. Partisan leader Runas suggested I should drop everything and join them, but I had seen their poor morale: they drank from despair and knew that sooner or later none of them would survive. I heard that the authorities at Leketschai had drawn up another indictment to deport me to eastern Siberia. Now I had my name on the reserve banishment list.

# 3

## *Banished to Siberia*

At 0500 hrs on 25 March 1949 I was woken by the forest warden. In winter I slept in the barn. Petrus told me that Toni had been informed she was to be banished to Siberia with her children. This involved me. After a long, heartfelt struggle I had decided that I could not abandon her to her fate. She was forty-four, nineteen years my senior. How would she cope alone without a man in the freezing wastes of Siberia? A year earlier I had made her a promise that I would share banishment with her. She had not believed this: 'When they come for me, you will run for it, just as many other men have done. They left even their wives and children in the lurch to save themselves from banishment.'

I was fearful of banishment, of the uncertainty of the destination and if I would ever return. Many died in banishment and the survivors only made enough to vegetate under the harsh work regime in the taiga. People died of the cold, and found their last rest in the expanses of Siberia, from the Arctic Sea to the taiga, the evergreen coniferous forests north of Mongolia, in the eternal permafrost. My father tried to dissuade me.

I went to Antoniena's dwelling. The NKVD guard would not let me enter, but their captain eventually relented. Toni sat on the bed crying, her smallest child, born in 1943, on her knee. I told her I was coming with her. She pleaded: 'Bruno, you know where they are sending me – Siberia! I beg you to reconsider so as not to regret it later.' The NKVD captain reminded me that I was still a young man – I could find a girl my own age to marry instead of this middle-aged woman with her three children. I asked him if Soviet people lived by choice in Siberia. He replied that it was an enormous undeveloped region of the Soviet Union.

Well then, I told him, if others can live there, so will I. I did have an ulterior motive, of course, in that the NKVD would sooner or later arrest me because of my contacts with the resistance. This would bring other things to the surface, including my service as a sniper with the German Wehrmacht. Once they had proof of that I could expect to face the firing squad. Thus I needed to make myself scarce, as had been suggested on more than one occasion before this.

Next the Soviet officer objected that my name did not appear on the banishment list, nor was I the man to whom Antoniena was presently married. He would allow me to travel, however, if I wrote a petition stating that I volunteered for banishment. Toni drafted it and I signed it. An exception was made for us on this basis – we could take along all our possessions. All other banished persons were restricted to what could be loaded on a lorry carrying four families. We had a lorry at our sole disposal, in which we could pack everything we salvaged after a final round of scavanging.

The lorries stood ready at Leketschai, the collection point for 'banishees'. A number of women were crying, they did not want to board the lorries. Many fell to their knees and begged the soldiers to shoot them. They did not want to be buried in the eternal permafrost of Siberia. They were then tossed into the lorries. At the railway station our train stood waiting and we boarded our specially adapted cattle truck. Possessions went below the floor, passengers journeyed inside. Barbed wire at the windows prevented escapes in transit. The doors were barred shut from outside and could not be opened by the occupants. A cubicle near the door contained a large bucket for personal needs. Whether one liked it or not, and the women in particular found it an embarrassment, everybody had to resort to this bucket. In the centre of the wagon was an iron stove with coal strewn near it.

Next morning the train stopped at Vilnius. Toni cried. Her elder son Ronas was a student at the university here. He knew nothing of the banishment of his mother, brother and sister to Siberia. The wagon doors were opened and a number of men and women climbed in. They had been banished after internment for varying periods in Lithuanian prisons for being in some way implicated with the resistance. They had no possessions apart from a small bundle.

Our train now left at great speed for Russia. At a stop far east of Moscow the wagon doors were opened again. On the third day we were allowed to alight to empty our bucket and fetch water. We were permitted to walk about inside a ring of guards armed with rifles and fixed bayonets. The train then continued for a stretch and halted in a large station where bread and tureens of hot soup were served, along with coal to stoke the stoves. Milk was handed out for the children and a female doctor visited each truck to ask if anybody was sick. During the journey one of the women gave birth. At the next station an ambulance stood ready to take the woman to the maternity ward. The train then left, her two small children remaining aboard – their distress can be imagined.

Once across the Urals into Asia, the guard was lessened. It was still winter and the snow lay in high drifts. We were allowed out for sanitary purposes at all stops. The facilities were multi-seaters, men and women sitting back to back. Sentries were posted nearby. An imprudent incident occurred. A certain place had been approved for emptying our latrine buckets. In one particular wagon, one of the girls emptied the bucket over the NKVD guard at the doorway. Everybody enjoyed the spectacle. The soldier was not authorised to leave his post and had to stand where he was, excrement running down his greatcoat and rifle. He cleaned his face with a cloth. At the change of guard the captain appeared and requested the culprit to step forward. Nobody did, and the girl was not given away. Then came the reprisals. The wagon door was locked shut for three days. The occupants received no warm soup, bread or water. Later the wagon was uncoupled and shunted into a siding for re-routing to the Arctic North.

Our journey into the unknown continued: Chelebinsk, Omsk, Krasnoyarsk, then Taishet and finally Irkutsk, north of Central Mongolia, where we detrained with all our belongings. A doctor checked if anybody was sick.

Lorries stood waiting to transport us onwards. The journey from Lithuania to Irkutsk had lasted four weeks. We spent more time stationary than under way. Old people sitting near us had given us lice and I itched everywhere. (I remembered that at the front in the trenches in summer when it was quiet we would undress and hunt for lice, cracking hundreds with our thumbnails.) The lorries moved out through frozen scenery. It was late April and Lake Baikal sparkled in the lights of the city. We were told at school that this was the world's deepest inland lake. German PoWs built the hydro-electric plant at Irkutsk and thousands paid for it with their lives.

We could no longer proceed by day: the sun was warm and the ground churned under the wheels. Winters here were cold and spring came suddenly, the warmth bringing a rapid thaw. Our journey was 450 kilometres to the key town of Rayon Shiegalva. There was no ashphalted highway; the lorries got bogged down in the mud. We had to wait for nightfall and the frost to freeze the earth again. Toni and I strolled through the taiga forest edges until it grew dark and the moon rose.

We drove on – taiga and more taiga. A village. Past settlements. Half-ruined villages. Abandoned hamlets. Here, in the collectivisation of the years 1932 to 1934, people were left to starve or were murdered for offering resistance in the communes. I feared for us if this was where we were to be settled. The fields were a wilderness surrounded by taiga forest and more taiga. There were places in the region untrodden by human foot, except perhaps for some lone hunter. The wolf and the bear ruled the taiga, where there are often distances of 200 kilometres between villages. It was not an easy region to escape from.

We came to a half-ruined village with few inhabitants. It was called Federoshene. Here we were unloaded. Lodging was needed for fifteen families. The populace was informed that we were a consignment of Fascists, bandits and profiteers from Lithuania being required to atone for our guilt by honest labour. At the end of the village was a farmstead of sorts where a Russian woman gave us a room. Wherever we looked we saw poverty and misery, a place where hope had long been abandoned.

The landlady's son, twelve years old or so, went out looking for potatoes in the private plot. He returned with a couple of rotted tubers which he rinsed and placed on the top of the stove to bake. This stove was situated in the middle of the kitchen and was used for cooking, but more importantly to heat the house twenty-four hours a day and keep the family from freezing to death. They had no blankets or luxuries like that, just rags. Toni and I exchanged glances. Was this our future?

We brought all our belongings into our room. A bundle of washing had been stolen by the lorry driver. Villagers came to see the new people who were so rich and possessed so much. Toni had a hundred roubles, I had nothing. We were supposed to be paid 400 roubles at the beginning of April for the month of March to start us off. So far we had seen none of it. The landlady provided hot water for a sauna to delouse, and then we went to bed. Unfortunately when the petrol lamp was lit the bed bugs came out to suck our blood. We danced and scratched all night since sleep was impossible. It had been better in the cattle trucks, which had no bed bugs. In the morning our faces were tired and drawn. We were summoned to the collective office where we had to surrender all our documents and identity papers. Those of us from Lithuania were now informed of our period of banishment. Toni's sentence was for life. Any attempt to escape would be punished by eight years in a forced-labour camp. From now on we belonged to the commandant and were obliged to obey all his orders. We could not go anywhere without the permission of the commandant, we had to obey the brigade commander and the collective manager and do all the work required. After signing a form that this had been explained to us, we were dismissed. Many left the office in tears. We were condemned to spend our whole lives here.

Initially we were in the charge of a commandant, who was aided by two militiamen; after a month an auxiliary commandant replaced him. This charming gentleman was called Poleko.

# 4

## *Labouring to Atone*

Spring came quickly, and we were put to work day and night to get the fields ploughed and sown. The earth thawed about fifty centimetres down, beneath that was the permafrost, so that even in summer the soil was cold. As nature awoke with the spring so did millions of mosquito-like midges, bloodthirsty little insects that bit the face and caused eyes and lips to swell up. One had to button up completely despite the heat and wear a face-net. Spring in the taiga was a wonderful season in which all kinds of tulips and flowers bloomed, but the plague of midges, and gadflies during the day, circled endlessly, awaiting the opportunity to suck blood.

There was a nearby river that was very rich in fish. This provided the staple protein of the populace, but the cow was the preferred provider. When a cow died, they all mourned, for then they would go short of milk and have none to put in their English-style cups of tea. When our landlady cooked, the scraggy dog would wait hungrily for a chance to lick the plate.

The working day was rewarded with half a kilo of flour and one-fifth of a rouble. It was a seven-day week. In the fields we were pestered endlessly by the midges and gadflies. In hot weather when one sweated it was awful, but on cloudy days or when it rained, it was infinitely worse. To be caught without a face-net was a fate worse than death. At night the bed bugs hit us. We scalded our bedding and the wooden bed frame. This forced the bugs to retreat to the ceiling, from where they dropped down on us while we slept. We did get accustomed to it slowly but it was not easy. If we slept in the meadow, we spent the night covered with fir branches and bark torn from the trees, and at night lit a fire to ward off the midges.

The collective farm provided us with food. If a hunter had caught a bear, the flesh was cooked for us and served with meal and potatoes. Soup was always available. Everything was costed and found to be valued at 2.5 roubles per serving. Since I only earnt one-fifth of a rouble daily I had to work more than a week for one meal. We were slaves and received just enough for a bare existence. Once I had a shock at harvest time. I had no cup and laid myself out at the stream to drink water. I heard a companion arrive to do the same, but when I glanced up to my horror I saw that I had a great bear for company. He was as shocked as I was and after a parting roar ran off for the taiga.

At four in the morning we were woken to scythe and gather wheat. At ten we breakfasted and rested for an hour before resuming cutting and baling. We made great haystacks for overwintering. I soon picked it up and became a master of the art.

We were opposed to many standard instructions. I argued that our Lithuanian girls should not have to get up at four, but at eight. Commandant Poleko arrived and beat me with a stick. I relieved him of it and cast it aside. At that he drew his pistol and fired a shot, which took my cap off. The incident was witnessed by the head of the meteorological station. I was arrested and my wrists handcuffed behind my back. My face-net was removed. I was taken the eighteen kilometres to the Federoshene collective, where a charge was drawn up. On the orders of Commandant Pfiliapenko I was forced to walk to Shiegalva, sixty-eight kilometres away. Polekon escorted me on his horse. I was the first of the 'banished' to be arrested. Toni cried and kissed me goodbye. It was the general opinion that I would be shot.

Late in the evening we arrived at Snaminka, where Poleko locked me in the jail. Dead tired, I was handcuffed by one wrist to the window bars in such a way that I could not lie down and had to spend the night standing up. I slept a little leaning against the wall, something I had learnt to do in the Wehrmacht. Whoever had a desperate need to sleep would be propped up left and right by two comrades so that he could sleep while on the march. After his turn he would help another to do the same.

Next morning the handcuffs were removed and I received some soup and bread. I had to march another sixty kilometres to Rayon Shiegalva, but the handcuffs were left off this time and I could fend off the midges from my face. We reached our destination next evening and I was put in the jailhouse to appear before the judge the next day. He thought I looked terrible and was sympathetic. I got five days' harsh confinement. My clothing was removed except for shirt and underpants and I was cast into a bug-infested dungeon. The only feature was a chair. The bugs soon found me and I kept picking them off my skin until my fingertips bled. I was exhausted, in total despair and suicidal. However, I could not reach the window bars, which were very high up, to end it all. I fell asleep. When I awoke next morning it was obvious what a feast the bugs had had all night. I was given half a cup of water and 200 grammes of bread. The water was nectar. The warders were not cruel and smuggled me soup and a full glass of water.

On the fifth day I was released. Very pallid, I could barely stand erect and went to the market place in the hope of selling my cape for bread. A man approached and asked if I were German. When I admitted it he invited me to the barrack hut he occupied with a woman and child. His name was Kerber, a Volga German, who had suffered cruelly in a forced-labour camp. He lived separated from his family and children. He gave me food and clothing although he had little for himself. Still very white, I began the two-day walk back to Antoniena. She advised me to guard my tongue in future: 'There is nothing you can do to change their arrogance and control,' she told me.

Harvest time had come. I was put to work scything, binding the corn and bringing it to the threshing machine. Threshing went on until three in the morning when we were given five hours' rest.

Now came autumn, the time to plant potatoes. Even the women and children were mobilised for the job. Fifteen hectares had to be sown with the contents of 200 sacks. The soil was very rich but had been neglected, and therefore yielded little. The seed potatoes were put in deep but the roots would have benefited from a bit of harrowing and ploughing, and did not flourish. Much remained to be done when the first night frost arrived on 5 September. We had to get a spurt on to plant our allotment and worked on our three hectares by night with the spade. We bartered our jackets for potatoes for immediate consumption.

A great deal of the land was unused, but if any was cultivated privately, dues were imposed. Toni cried. We had no funds to buy kerosene or salt. Where would the money come from? Already we had sold off our newly sewn jackets to avoid starvation. Some men who worked on the fields were too weak to walk home for lack of food after work and the lorry had to be sent to fetch them. The state's quota from each cow was eight kilos of butter, and from each hen sixty eggs. Failure to provide the quota meant condemnation as an enemy of the state and transfer to a forced-labour camp, where the death rate was enormous.

In the spring the cattle were of terribly gaunt appearance, having been overwintered outdoors, even at night, in temperatures of -50°C and below. How could a cow give milk when she was a mere bag of bones and her hide was peeling away? Many who drank the milk from the collective without boiling it fell sick. Several young men died in agony, lashed to the bed, there being no medicines.

In the summer of 1949, after the cereal harvest, the Hofer and Montvilas families decided to abscond back to Lithuania. They succeeded in getting away, but after a month of endless difficulties were arrested boarding a train, sent back and sentenced to a forced labour camp. It was pitiful to hear the crying of the little daughter when the families were broken up by order of the judge and the child sent to the orphanage at Tipta.

At Oblush in the eastern neighbourhood of Irkutsk it began to snow early. We had not yet managed to get the harvest under cover before it was covered by snow. Elderly people, who got little to eat, had a high mortality rate during this season. I dug graves for more than one in the eternal permafrost of the cemetery. The earth had to be heated with fire before the spade would go in.

Initially the inhabitants had looked upon us with mistrust. They had been told we were enemies of the state, profiteers and Fascists who sucked the life blood of others. Their opinions changed quickly when they saw that the Lithuanians at least were a very industrious people, unlike many Russians, whose men shied from work and drank all day. This was particularly the case with those who had come back from the war.

A commission arrived from Rayon Shiegalva. The chairman and party secretary wanted to check how much wheat we had over. Their quota under the state plan had been increased to compensate for a shortfall from other collectives. The reason was that they had met their targets and reported the fact to Moscow. The collective workers had no bread and were starving, but this was of no interest to the commission, whose only interest was the state's quota. If necessary they would take whatever the collective members had for their own personal needs to meet the quota. The members, being slaves, had no rights and were not actually entitled to own anything.

Eastern Siberia had a rich soil. If the land had belonged to Lithuanian farmers they would have turned it into a paradise. However, for the communists, who were not interested in people, the possibilities were closed to their limited minds. Before the Bolshevik Revolution the Russian people were wealthy and propertied. They harvested so much that their barns overflowed with wheat to the extent that they were at a loss what to do with it all. But now, under a superficial system of 'husbandry', a communist hectare yielded 500 kilos of wheat as opposed to a possible eight tonnes using good farming methods.

The state plan was the bugbear. First, the quota imposed on the state farms and collectives had to be met. Then they had to pay for the seeds the state had lent them for wheat in the spring, and not forgetting the dues to the tractor unit for the loan of 'the technology'. All meat and butter had to be rendered up to the state. Each worker received 600 grammes of grain for bread. The remuneration was subject to taxes and other deductions such as 'insurance', leaving a net daily income from the year's profit of about a fifth of a rouble, enough for one person to buy himself a meal every ten days.

Settlement Day was usually held in February. Everyone had to turn out. A village band would play, and the village would be hung with red flags and banners bearing slogans that heaped praise on the Communist Party with thanks and adulation to Lenin, Stalin and Marx. The chairman and party secretary would be there. The latter would deliver an address and thank the farm workers for their endeavours and high output. On this occasion the chairman presented our state farm manager with the 'Superlative Flag', the highest distinction a collective could receive, indicating that it had exceeded its quota under the state plan. A prize of 1,000 roubles went with it, of which the collective activists received 60 per cent. Everybody clapped and applauded the wisdom of Stalin and the Communist Party, but all it meant for us was another year of starvation and stagnation. We also received sixty kilos of wheatmeal each to see us over the period from summer to autumn, when we worked seven days a week, twelve hours a day. I owed the collective 200 roubles for having needed to eat to keep up my strength to work.

Collective workers had no identity papers. It was strictly forbidden to let them have such documents for fear they might be used in escape attempts. We were registered to the chairman of the village community. Most of the young men conscripted into the Red Army settled elsewhere in the Soviet Union upon completion of their term of service. Those who went to the better schools also had the chance to escape this slavery. Thus the quality of the young in the villages became progressively poorer. A death would go unreported so that the family could benefit from the deceased's bread ration. When the body began to decompose it would be put into a clamp together with any others to await spring.

I went to the blockhouse and counted my potatoes. Would there be enough for today and tomorrow? I decided on having three today. I put a pot on the fire with the three potatoes, hacked away some frozen milk, and threw in a handful of flour. This was my lunch and supper. I put another pot containing snow on the iron stove, thawed it and boiled it for tea. That was my allowance. I had met the daily norm today and was exhausted. I was credited 2.5 workdays and had earnt 1.5 kilos of flour and three-fifths of a rouble. I lay down on the cart, covered myself with an overcoat, fell asleep and dreamt of home.

Christmas Eve 1949. The food was nearly all gone. I had to go to Toni at Federoshene. It was snowing, with a rising wind. I decided to walk the fifteen kilometres rather than wait for the sledge in the morning. I left at midday, calculating I could make it by nightfall. The wind blew fiercer, but in the taiga forests one did not notice it so much. When I came out of the taiga and made my way crosscountry the last couple of miles to Federoshene, there was forty-five degrees of frost and the wind burnt my cheeks and face. I was walking directly into it – progress ahead was hard going. I grew weary, became too weak and dropped. The village was barely a kilometre away but I was done for. Beneath the glittering stars I had a vision as the wind and snow combined to bury me. It was easy this way and I no longer felt the cold.

---

Two hunters came along with their dogs. The animals barked and began to paw at the snowdrift. I was found. The men bore me, unconscious and stiff, to their dwelling, rubbed me over with snow and revived me. Their sustained effort saved my life. With a mouthful of vodka to keep me going, they brought me to Toni, who fainted when I came to the door. The doctor was called from Suaminko. I had a high fever and double pneumonia. My feet and face were frozen, but recovered without frostbite having set in. There were large wounds on my feet, which were not healing. I was taken to the hospital at Shiegalva, to the surgeon Lapko. They wanted to amputate my feet, but Lapkov said, 'If he is against it, we can wait a bit.' I had lost sensation in some of my toes, but the feeling returned slowly. After a month I was back with Toni at Federoshene. Once again death had passed me by.

# 5

## *Removal to Rudovka, April 1950*

Commandant Fielebenko came in March 1950. We had to sign every month to prove we were still there. Because the Federoshene collective farm could not feed all the banishees, it was decided to transfer out five families. Toni and I were to move to the Molotov collective at Rudovka. The lorries came for us in April. Rudovka was ten kilometres from Rayon Shiegalva on the river Lena. We were given a house that had been occupied previously by a geological expedition. Under the floorboards we found about five hundredweight of frozen potatoes that had not cooked well. This was a gift to us, together with the iron stove in the middle of the room. The stove had to be kept going day and night for us to survive the cold.

We were subordinated to Commandant Gemshieko. We slaves belonged to him from now on and had to sign to the effect that we would not leave the village without his permission to go to Shiegalva, which was more like civilisation, having a hospital, doctors and shops, unlike Federoshene, which had nothing. Everybody came to stare. Word had got round that rich profiteers with many possessions had arrived. Even the chairman came, although his primary interest was Antoniena's daughter Grashina, who was becoming a very pretty girl.

They gave me a plane and saws to fashion a table and two benches. We made the beds, but as soon as dark fell the bugs came out and attacked. It was impossible to sleep and in the morning we all had headaches. We spent all next day boiling water and pouring scalding water into every crack. Next day I went into Shiegalva and bought a proprietary powder from the pharmacist to mix with quicklime. With this I painted the interior of the house and exterminated all the bugs. It was queer how all Russian dwellings were bug-ridden.

Output was not so good as at Federoshene. One person who had been banished to Rudovka was Jenshai. His father had worked in the United States and put some money by. He had bought twenty-five hectares, built a house on it and so had some property. This got him condemned as a profiteer and he was banished. When he died I made his coffin and buried him in the cemetery. I once asked his son Jonas: 'Why were you banished? You fought with the Soviet Army.' He had been conscripted in 1944. He told me:

> We took a Regimental Staff prisoner. Even today I cannot get over how they just surrendered when we told them to. They laid their weapons aside. They were interrogated, the Soviet officers liked their clothing: furs, leather coats and boots, also the decorations the Oberst and his officers wore. They wanted them. They ordered the soldiers to take the officers out to a hole to be shot. We led them out and forced them to undress. A Major took off his clothing with a look of disdain for us, the others then followed. When they were in their shirts and underwear, the eight officers were shot, murdered.

He told me he had been unable to forget that this had no military purpose, it was done for greed and to steal. All his life he would remember the look of contempt the Germans had given their assassins. He had opened his mouth once too often and finished up here.

In the spring the cows looked awful because they had been overwintered outdoors. Only those with calf were brought into the cowstalls. The remainder shivered through every long, bitterly cold night. Each morning they were driven to the river to drink. The water flowed from a spring and never froze. There was no feed for cattle, of course. The hide peeled off many of them and the ensuing cull would be considered a necessary event and the meat eaten. We lived near the farm and got the lungs and liver when we helped strip the hide.

At a meeting it was proclaimed that anybody could set up as a collective farmer in his own right – *Kolchosnink*. One would then receive the hectare around his house as his own property. Those who declined would receive one-quarter of a hectare to grow potatoes for domestic use. Goga the Lithuanian and I volunteered. Everybody thought it was very funny that we had sold ourselves out to spend the rest of our lives here as *Kolchosnink*.

In Lithuania the cattle stood around the house and so the earth was well manured. To find black soil on the Lena one had to dig down one metre. Mixed with loam and worked in right, it would yield sixteen tonnes of potatoes per hectare. I teamed up two horses and ploughed forty *are* (1 are = 119.6 square yards). A crowd looked on as I took a spade and put some sprouted tubers and eyes in the furrows about five centimetres deep and covered them over with earth. They all laughed and said, 'It's too hot here, the sun will burn them all up.' But I had served a farm apprenticeship under Arno Braemer at Fichtenhöhe and other farmers from my childhood. When my father fell ill, I became a farm worker and put what I had learnt to good use. I grew up on a farm and carried out all manner of tasks until I was conscripted into the Wehrmacht in 1943. I certainly knew about how to grow potatoes.

The Russians in this region sowed their potatoes really deep, close to the permafrost. The potatoes spent ages in the ground and rarely germinated because it was too cold. I saw that at Federoshene. As soon as the potatoes came up the worms went for them. One could hardly call it a harvest when on average a hectare yielded less than a tonne. In Lithuania we would reap at least three to four tonnes per hectare if the job was done anywhere near right. In the collectives the state plan said fifty hectares to potatoes. The managers dictated everything and wanted no new-fangled nonsense.

My potatoes in the ploughed meadow soon began to show. I hoed morning and evening. They grew quickly and the turned sods of earth rotted into manure below. The forty *are* I had sown in winter turned into a harvest of 117 large sacks. I worked on the collective farm during the day and harvested my own potatoes at night by the light of the moon until the first night frosts eight degrees below occurred between 7 and 10 September. In our garden Toni and Grashina planted cucumbers, onions, cabbage and beetroot. We were the only house to grow large red tomatoes. We had a hundred plants. People came from all around, including those who had laughed at us, to see our garden. We had all the potatoes we could possibly need and no longer went hungry. From our sales we acquired all our necessities, including petrol for the lamp, and sugar. We also stitched jackets padded with cotton wadding.

Rye, wheat and barley had to be harvested. The ground was all soft with the rain, and the mud clung to the wheels of every vehicle. Reaping was done with hoes, scythes and sickles. We worked a twelve-hour day every day of the week. The collective was behind on its quota. On the Sunday a lorry arrived from Shiegalva bringing the harvesters from the factories. Overnight and early morning it rained torrentially after heavy storms and there was water everywhere. The Rayon Shiegalva manager, commandant and party secretary came to exhort the banishees to keep at it.

The wheat, bound in sheaves, was brought to the threshing machine. I had to put the soaking-wet sheaves into the machine. This caused the ears to be rammed into the haulm. I stopped the machine and took a half-threshed sheaf to the Rayon manager and said it was impossible to thresh because the corn went into the straw. He ordered me to keep threshing. I lost my temper and told him that we collective farmers would go without bread again. We were being told to do the impossible to meet the quota so that they would all get a medal, and nobody cared if the collective farmers starved. At that the commandant ordered my arrest, and I was taken at once to Shiegalva in handcuffs like a common criminal.

In the jail I was beaten with rubber-coated coshes until my back was black and blue and bled from open weals. With these wounds, and my hands still restrained, I was re-acquainted with the same bug-infested cell as before. I lost consciousness on the concrete floor.

I had committed a capital offence. In the Soviet Union, if one uttered a criticism witnessed by three communists prepared to testify to it in writing, the accused would be brought before a judge the same night. Stalin had issued an edict that the offence carried the death penalty, which would be executed without any plea in mitigation being heard. There was no advocate, no appeal and no stay of execution. The NKVD had to carry out the sentence within twenty-four hours.

Upon regaining consciousness, hands bound, and handcuffed too, I staggered to my feet with my last ounce of strength. I wanted to die. The bugs had feasted on my blood, my eyes were bulging from their sockets. My tongue stuck to the roof of my mouth, I had no saliva. I was desperate for water, but none came. Most probably they thought I would be brought before the judge Monday and shot as an enemy of the people and state. It no longer mattered to me. I hoped merely that my end would be swift. Death would come as a relief.

Around midday my cell door was opened. The Rayon manager and the commandant stood before me. They said they were really sorry, for I was a good worker, but I had to learn to curb my tongue. The commandant ordered my restraints to be removed. I was sent home so as to continue working that night.

My clothing was returned and I left with mixed feelings. After downing a glass of water, weak on my feet, I set off for Rudovka, ten kilometres distant. Most of the weals on my back had burst and the wounds caused my shirt to stick. When Toni saw my condition she told me: 'You are so stupid. You were their guest for the second time in a year. The third time will be the last. Everybody knows you have to keep quiet. It is only you who simply has to have his say. When will you recognise that we can do nothing, we are slaves!' Later that day she told me she was pregnant. Now I had a reason for living. I would sacrifice myself to ensure my child had a future. Despite all the hardship and misery in banishment, Toni looked foward with joy to the prospect of another child. I clung to her. I had nobody else in life. As a woman she was my wife and mother. She had become my life-partner who spared no effort to educate me and get me to make something of myself, a simple village boy.

Soon it was time for the collective to harvest the potato crop. All the women, even the old ones, had to lend a hand. Five *ares* was the norm and 1.25 workdays were credited. The potatoes were soft. In my garden, which had been ploughed before sowing and I had hoed to keep the weeds down, I dug out one plant that yielded eighteen large tubers, three handfuls. By moonlight I filled 317 sacks from four-tenths of a hectare. The fifteen hectares of the collective bore only 280 sacks, not enough to repay the seed potatoes the state had lent for planting – a pointless exercise.

In the spring I had to go into the taiga – still snowbound – to saw and prepare wood for the schools, the hospital and other official centres. The norm was set at five cubic metres for two men over 1.5 workdays. Working with two saws, I fulfilled the norm by myself and also felled a tree with the axe. At another place

I cut down more than a hundred metres for winter and sold a portion. I had no help. I wanted to work and had to work in order to secure the life of my family in banishment. At night I went to mow hay where the collectives had neglected to burn it off. I dried it and carried it home on my back, and sold it in Shiegal a later in the winter.

The harvest went on into the winter. The wheat standing in the fields had to be scythed down. The threshing machines worked all night, lorries conveying the dried cereal day and night to Shiegalva for the state. They raised our quota further under the plan. The last lorries were adorned with red flags, people played the harmonica. Slogans of praise were strung up with the edifying news that our harvest was on its way to our teachers, the Great Communist Party and our wise Stalin. He was our father. With joy and gratitude we were being led into a happy future towards which Communism showed us the path. After the books were balanced the collective farmers were left with nothing save some grain in payment for the day.

Toni and I made a feather mattress. We sold it in Shiegalva for a goat that we named Mune. She bore two kids, of which one was slaughtered. She gave us milk to add to our morning tea and also to enrich our potato soup together with some flour. We were very well off, for we had bread to eat in the morning and potatoes in the evening. We ate only twice per day.

When the financial adjuster came, we had a serious problem. We used a *Kolchosnink* hectare, of which 1.5 *are* was for vegetables and forty *ares* for potatoes. This was assessed for 1,200 roubles tax. Where on earth would we get such a sum? Our outgoings exceeded our miserable earnings. We could not meet the monthly instalment and so they confiscated the goat. Toni cried. She was malnourished and the milk from the goat was important for us. A woman lent us milk. On the Sunday we went to market: amongst other things I sold my last suit to cancel our debt and we got the goat back.

Christmas Eve 1950 came: we covered our Christmas table with everything we had: beetroot, boiled potatoes and sauerkraut. Toni put aside a half-litre of goat's milk. We were rich again. Others did not do so well and went hungry. We lit papers on the wall, stood in the shadows and tried to divine the future. Everybody was thinking of home. Toni was crying, remembering her eldest son Romas, who had been spared banishment because he had been at university on 25 March 1949. Penniless, he had been thrown out of university. Now and again relatives sent him sausages and ham.

I wanted to go to the taiga to fetch a wooden sled I had made there. On the way a pack of wolves came for me. My horse reared up and I had trouble holding her. My only weapon was the axe. The female wolf, a young, fine animal, came within three metres to size me up while the remainder of the pack, about twenty animals, held back. It was strange – I had no fear and suddenly got the idea they were just looking. The wolf and I exchanged stares as though we understood each other, and then they left. I wiped the sweat from my forehead.

I had been paid two sacks of wheat for labour and went to the water-mill at Nisne Ilabadga, twenty-eight kilometres from Rudovka. The wheat was milled for bread there. The miller was a Lithuanian banishee. The collective gave me three sacks to take. The track went through the taiga to the Shiegalva–Balaginsk/Irkutsk fork: from the fork it was three kilometres to the mill. I had to wait a day for my turn. As I was feeding the horse, the miller told me, 'Take this pot and two rags to bind to a stick to make a torch because you have no gun.' (Banishees were not allowed to carry arms.) 'If you get attacked by wolves, light a torch. They are frightened of fire.' He shook some petrol on a cloth to show me how. I had my axe and doubted that a torch would be much good.

I got my flour and pulled out that afternoon. Along the track to Shiegalva a snowstorm set in with an icy wind. All the paths were covered over and I could see no trace of the road. I put my trust in the horse to get me and the cargo back. Her hooves would detect the track and find the way. She got me to the taiga despite many difficulties. The icy wind carried large snowflakes and whipped my face; I had to keep rubbing my nose and cheeks to prevent frostbite. I got off and walked behind the sled, for the horse had enough to pull without my weight as well. In the bitter cold I was worried at my lack of warm winter clothing.

From afar I saw the light of the wolves' eyes, which glittered in the dark. The pack waylaid me; this time I felt sure they would attack. Forgoing the axe, I saw that it was a matter of life and death that I lit the torch. In the high wind with trembling fingers it was no easy task. Finally I got it burning and ran at the wolves, waving it from side to side. They retreated, and the horse plodded forward with the sled, using the last vestiges of her strength. I arrived at Rudovka at midnight, dripping with sweat despite the cold. The horse had got us home. Toni cried when she saw me come back. In her heart she had anticipated the danger when I left. I had sensed her love and care and had not felt alone. I had to be there for the future.

Winter had come again. We scythed the last of the wheat from the snowfields. By the beginning of November, all the fieldwork was completed.

In Shiegalva I met some former Waffen-SS men. They told me about a railway branch line from Taishet to Uskat on the Lena which had been laid by German PoWs, forced labour from punishment camps, and Russians who had been prisoners of the Germans. The worst treated were members of the Vlassov Army, who were singled out for particular cruelty. Thousands upon thousands died. In the permafrost below every hump, far from home, lie five or six banishees. The trains roll out with freight for the North over their bones.

The Volga Germans from the Crimea and Odessa had been placed in the Warthegau in eastern Germany by the Resettlement Commission with German–Soviet agreement in 1940. When the Poles took over the territory the Volga Germans were expelled with an allowance of forty-six kilos per person, all else being expropriated. All had finished up in banishment. I conversed with them a great deal. In Vorkuta and Norilsk, as slaves, they built the Arctic Road – malnutrition and beatings claimed thousands of their lives. Building the locks on the Arctic Canal and the Koslosa–Vorkuta railway line also cost tens of thousands of German PoWs their lives; gravel and sand were shovelled over their corpses and the railway laid on top. The Soviet Union was a state in which cruelty was triumphant. Its slogan was: 'Workers of the World Unite', but even their own lived in fear of the terror the state wielded.

We still had enough to eat: bread and goat's milk, and received packets of sausage and ham from Toni's sister in Lithuania. The potato was our staple food. At Christmas 1950 Antoniena was pregnant. I wanted a son and joked about it with Toni. I drove every day into the taiga to saw wood for the school and bring home dry wood for ourselves, which I sawed by moonlight. Our living room was large and had to be heated day and night otherwise we would have frozen. The iron stove consumed a lot of firewood.

At the beginning of February 1951 we had a meeting to settle the accounts. The success of the past year was to be rewarded in money and kind. A hired orchestra came: we had to pay for it. The Rayon Shiegalva manager and the party secretary attended. The collective manager delivered the opening address praising the great service of 'our wise father and teacher Stalin'. Everybody stood up and clapped. We thought the eulogy would never end, so grateful was the speaker to him. We had met the quota of the state plan in wheat, meat, wool and butter. We received recognition for our good work, and I was even mentioned by name. Unfortunately, however, we had not maintained a great enough effort to get the harvest in during the long rains and much had been lost. Therefore, the best that could be offered for the coming year for a day's work was 800 grammes of wheat and one-twenty-eighth of a rouble. Our family, with daughter Grashina, had earnt 160 kilos of wheat but owed the collective 112 roubles. Now we had to tighten our belts again. All we had was the potato crop I had harvested by moonlight.

My son Vitautus was born at Shiegalva hospital on 1 June 1951. Toni had little breast milk but a neighbouring mother had excess and wet-nursed him.

In the winter of 1952 I got two good horses. In 1953 the state plan dictated that I should be responsible for fifteen hectares of potatoes. I was happy with this, provided they gave me a free hand. In the autumn of 1954 they decided I should take over the pig farm.

The collective had 148 sows with a number of midget weaners in appalling condition. The pig farm was a new feature and I was to be head man. I often had arguments with Toni about the time I was spending at work in the collective, which used up all my strength and energy. I had less time for our own garden and Toni was having to do more and more. She did not like this and asked me to take a little more interest in herself and the domestic business. She was right, but often I had work to do and obligations to be discharged. These resulted frequently in my coming home very late. Nobody in the collective could match my hours. We were paid 1.5 kilos of wheat for one workday at that time and I had 1,300 days' credit. I sold some of this wheat on the market and bought some porkers, as well as a battery-operated radio (because we had no electricity). We were the first family in Rudovka to have a radio.

We had done so well in four years that we were better off than the local inhabitants of the collective. It had all been achieved by our own efforts, by dedicated work. I worked day and night so that my family had a better standard of living than the others.

Christmas 1954 was the most joyful to date. On the radio we heard the 'Voice of America', reception being good here in the taiga. We listened to 'Bishop B.' in America, offering comfort and solace to those in distress, which gave us heart. We all cried. We remembered our families in the homeland who had not forgotten us, in Germany, Lithuania and the West. My son was three now. When somebody asked him 'What are you?' he would always reply 'a Fritz' and everybody laughed.

It was no laughing matter, however, when the barns stood empty and even the rats gave up looking for food there. They burrowed through to our house and ate our potatoes. In the dark they ran round the living room. Once Toni was woken up: Vitautas was in the cradle and a rat got to him and started nibbling, which woke him up. Toni screamed when she saw the size of the rat. They ran over our heads while we slept, they bit Toni's ears and pulled at her hair. I was bitten on the nose. One night when I caught one it bit my hand and I had to release it.

A Russian woman gave me a young cat and explained that none of the local Russians would live in our house because when the barns were empty the rats always moved into it. They would come out of their holes as we slept. The cat caught a big rat by the neck and would not let it go. The rat cried, so did the cat; I dived in to help. The rats decided it was getting too hot for them and evacuated the house. The little cat was very fond of me and liked to sit on my knees, her claws were quite gentle. She like to wrap herself around my neck or lie on my feet. She would always be waiting for me when I came home from work.

In the winter we had twelve hens under the kitchen table. In the spring we slaughtered the pigs. At night I would often listen to the radio – at three in the morning the BBC came through clear.

They broadcast in German for two hours. It was even possible to get 'Deutsche Welle' on medium wave, but it was much fainter. I heard the bells of Cologne Cathedral ringing in Christmas and New Year 1955.

# 6

## *A Soviet Piggery:*
## *I am Recognised as a German Sniper*

Antoniena and I were finding ourselves at odds ever more often.
She suspected, without foundation, that when I went to the accounts
office to write up the workdays for others, I was taking more than
a passing interest in Riana the book-keeper and spending too long
there. Actually I did not have time to stay in one place for long,
otherwise I could not allocate and control the work.

When I took over the pig farm in 1954, the women used to feed
the pigs all outdoors where it was easier to steal the pigs' food for
themselves. I realised that this could not go on. First, I kept a close
watch and divided up the herd so that each woman had thirty
pigs, breeding boars, sows and piglets, which they had to feed
themselves. A big cellar was built nearby to store potatoes in winter
against the severe frosts – there was space for a hundred tonnes.
One day a meeting was held at the piggery, during the course of
which I told the women that they had to obey my instructions
unconditionally. The conflict that had been simmering for some
time now came to a head when Mrs Naviskaya lobbed a bucket in
my direction. 'My son fell in the war. You Fascists killed him. In
Lithuania you sucked the people's blood. For that reason you were
banished here. You should not have been banished but shot. You
are not going to suck our blood!'

I went to the collective manager, Novopashendes, and told
him I was resigning from the pig farm. After my report the party
secretary went with me to confront the women: 'If you do not want
to work in the piggery, we will replace you. You are required to
obey all Sutkus's instructions. We know he was a German soldier –

state organs are taking it up. It has nothing to do with you.' Thus I remained at my post.

The pig farm had a serious technical problem because all the stock was inbred. Nobody had thought of switching the sows round with other piggeries each year in a proper breeding policy. I had to explain to the collective board that it was necessary to start over from the beginning, and why. After hearing me out, even the Rayon chairman was on my side. Thus I accompanied the manager of the collective from one farm to another exchanging boars and breeding sows. This led to further major unpleasantness – now it was said that Sutkus wanted to sell off the herd, and I was denounced to the authorities. The procurator came from the state attorney's office to examine the matter but found no irregularities.

The pig farm recovered, and sows were soon producing litters of eleven to twelve piglets, and these looked in much better shape than anything previously. Beforehand, when they were weaned at one month, they looked poorly and the death rate was high. Once I renewed the bloodline all piglets from a litter survived.

I kept the good young sows, culled the older ones and let the state have them since they cost the farm money and made no profit. My piggery soon became the most profitable branch of the collective. The woman responsible for the pigs stayed in the sty when a sow farrowed to make sure the mother did not squash any of the young because after the eleventh live birth the attendant kept the twelveth as a prize. I maintained the log, and in one month some of the women worked the equivalent of 114 workdays.

Antoniena's daughter Grashina had grown. She was allowed to attend the ninth and tenth grade of secondary school at Shiegalva. There were pupils there from Krughai in Lithuania. I did everything I could to aid her education.

I was ordered to a state farm at the village of Voryoba. In summer they cultivated the fields and in winter went into the taiga to fell trees, which were then stacked by the Lena. In the spring the trunks were rafted down-river to Shiegalva where they were used for house-building or would be loaded later for other purposes with freight for the tundra in the North.

Few people could survive in the Arctic Circle. Most fell ill with *zenga* or scurvy. Their teeth fell out, they suffered from dysentry and only the strongest survived. Many Volga Germans finished up there, especially at Norilsk, the arctic city. Propaganda boasted that it had been built by Soviet labour, but of course it had been made by hundreds of thousands of men from the forced-labour camps who died there building it and the factories.

Voryoba was thirty-five kilometres from Rudovka. I had to load the felled trees on my horse-drawn sled at the taiga and take them to the Lena. For this I received half my accredited wage, the collective got the rest – the work involved two days' pay for each day worked.

I was given lodgings with an old woman and my horses were kept in her corral. I had to rise at four each morning to feed them, harness them up at six and then make my way fifteen kilometres uphill to the log stands. I had to go even when the temperature was -50°C, when the frost bit so deeply that glass splintered. The old lady laboured under a great sorrow. Her husband had been led off in 1937 for uttering some criticism or other and had never been heard from again. All her seven sons had fallen for Russia on the German front. She showed me their photos and wept. The youngest, barely eighteen, had died in the final battle for Berlin. Every night she made his bed and unmade it each morning. Although she knew I had been a German soldier, she adopted me as her son and gave me her boys' winter clothing, since she had no further need of it. Anna Federovna is now long gone, but she lives on in my heart.

I moved all the wood, then I went back with my horses to Rudovka. I found it very difficult to part from my adoptive Russian mother. She gave me her blessing and wished me a homecoming to Germany one day. I should not forget her, she said, even if I were thousands of miles away from the taiga on the Lena.

I was needed at home. The supplies of wood I had managed to bring from the taiga earlier had been exhausted and more was required. So I loaded the sled with straw and went to Shiegalva, where people who kept cattle could use it. I sold it to a German family and took tea with them. They were astonished to learn that I had been a German soldier; they had lived in a colony in Odessa. In 1940 the German–Soviet Repatriation Commission moved them to Torenz in the Warthegau, but when the area was overrun by the Russians, the Poles kicked the Germans out. This resulted in the Russian commandant having to take measures against the Poles to protect the Volga Germans. The latter were all rounded up into camps and later deported to Uzbekistan. The children of the family were all under fourteen. The grandparents were forced to work in the rice paddies and also picked cotton. They died there, as did the children, of diphtheria, malaria and typhus. People dropped like flies. Only this couple survived. The wife had found out that her husband had fought in the Waffen-SS but survived. The Russians had put him to work on the Koslo kabis–Vorkuta railway line from where he returned a physical wreck. The woman cried: she had lost everything, her parents, her children, and her husband was in poor health. It was a tragedy.

On my return I drove through the village of Galanovka, where a Lithuanian acquaintance, Shakotes, lived. We conversed, and I confided that I was German and had fought in the Wehrmacht as a sniper. Unfortunately his son was an informer for the Soviet Committee for the Secret Service and next day was in possession of all the facts I had related to the father. Other informants, such as Petras Kunieska, who pretended to have been with the Lithuanian Resistance, came to glean what they could. Antoniena warned me, 'Don't chatter so much. You never know who these people really are!'

I noticed that I had become a person of interest for the KGB. Now others came to probe. By then we had had the radio for several years and used to listen to 'Voice of America'. The KGB knew this too. One day the chairman of the community visited Antoniena discreetly, wanting to know who and what I really was. She gave him a sharp rebuff and sent him on his way.

In February 1956 I was summoned before Commandant Haushikov at Shiegalva. He had with him a KGB officer, Schveitsov, from the administrative offices at Irkutsk. He was very courteous. He placed on the table before me three photographs showing me in the presence of General der Panzertruppe FritzHubert Gräser, C-in-C, 4. Panzer-Armee, as his guest of honour. They had a number of other files from the captured archives of the German Wehrmacht. Confronted by this evidence, I could not deny that I was the sniper Obergefreiter Bruno Sutkus.

Schveitso said: 'We have known for some time who you are. Your trial had already begun!' Later I discovered that they intended to try me before a military court on the charge of being a war criminal, but after the first West German federal chancellor, Konrad

Adenauer, was received in Moscow, the trial was abandoned and I was granted amnesty. Schveitso told me that I had been extremely lucky and had 'got away with it by the skin of my teeth'. 'If we had found you out earlier, you would be dead now. You were lucky, banishment bought you the time you needed,' he said.

Of course, a Soviet amnesty was not the same as anybody else's amnesty, as I was to find out. The commandant told me that on the basis of this amnesty, I was to be discharged from the collective. This required the authority of a membership meeting in the presence of all the members. Only then would I receive the discharge document. In Rudovka I showed Toni my amnesty certificate, which would enable me to obtain identity papers after the membership meeting, provided they agreed. The district chairman was at the meeting and said that Antoniena had to apply to return to Lithuania, and if she did so they would also consider her period of banishment remitted. Then they would release me from the collective. At that Toni grasped my hand and we left the assembly – in what was considered an overly demonstrative manner.

Antoniena had rented half a house with six *ares* of garden with Marina, an inhabitant of Shiegalva, and had paid 800 roubles in advance for six months. We moved in. I was sorry to leave Rudovka. I had rather got used to the place and had bought my own house there. It was the first property I had ever owned. We had sold the house in Rudovka and moved to Shiegalva early one morning, without the permission of the collective. However, I could get no work in Shiegalva because I had no release document from the Rudovka collective. Thus I had to return to see the chairman of the district. He gave me a fierce lecture: who did I think I was, making a dramatic exit before all the farmers of the collective at the meeting? In his opinion my guilt outweighed anybody else's. I was an assassin and should be hanged – shooting was too good for me. As far as he was concerned there was no amnesty, and I had to return to Rudovka to continue working there. He would certainly not be supplying any document enabling me to obtain identity papers. I told him I would not return to his collective, and at that he threw me out of his office.

Now I was at a loss. I went to the flour-collective combine at the mill and asked if they needed wood for the locomotive. Few men were prepared to enter the green hell of the taiga in summer to saw wood where millions of midges and mosquitoes and swarms of gadflies were waiting to suck blood. However, I had no other solution. Better the green hell of the taiga than back to the collective at Rudovka.

Next morning I was working with two others in the taiga. Our job was to saw strips of wood 70 cm x 140 cm long. We were paid seven roubles for each cubic metre of wood cut to that size. I sawed eight cubic metres in fouteen hours with my handsaw. I felled the trees with the axe. It was a ghastly experience to have to work buttoned up and wearing a stocking mask drawn over the face to prevent the insects biting eyes and lips. On hot days the gadflies would circle like a swarm of bees. The worst thing was not being able to wipe away the sweat. I knuckled down to it and in the first month received 120 roubles – after seven years' forced labour in the collective it was the first real money I had earnt. I bought Toni material for a silky dress, which a Lithuanian seamstress sewed together for her. It was the first time I had bought her a present since we had been here in banishment. My small son Vitautus also got a new suit, and there was enough over for a shirt for me.

Each night we got about four hours' sleep in an old blockhouse. I would rise very early. We went out to saw wood while it was still dark and worked until late in the night. Then I would return to the blockhouse, set the fire, cook and eat. Meat, flour, potatoes and bread formed my diet. Afterwards I would sink down in exhaustion on the floorboards, which for me were like a soft bed, and sleep four hours during the worst of the heat. Then I sawed and chopped again the next day until late evening.

After three weeks I left the taiga. Toni and Vitautus were at the Shiegalva hospital – the doctors had found renal calculus. The boy cried terribly when the attacks came. An air ambulance was ordered from Irkutsk. Next day when they operated, the surgeon noticed evidence of spinal tuberculosis in the fifth and sixth vertebrae, and Vitautus was admitted to the Hospital for Infantile Tuberculosis at Irkutsk. He remained interned for more than a year and was confined day and night to a plaster cast until his spine healed.

# 7

## *Soviet Bureacracy in Action*

The police ordered me to sort out the business with my papers as soon as possible, since I could not remain in Shiegalva without identity documents. I was to seek work with a proper organisation and not rove the taiga.

Cap in hand I went before the Rayon chairman again. This time he gave me a generous welcome and did not boot me out as he had done the previous year. He instructed his female secretary to prepare a certificate, which, bearing his signature, gave me the right to obtain my identity document.

At the office which issued ID the major requested my old ID and proof that I was a German born in East Prussia. If I could furnish my original birth certificate and ID issued by the Third Reich, proving my German nationality, they would issue me with a stateless person's ID. This was because I had a Lithuanian document (forged, unknown to them) denying that I was German and affirming that I was stateless. They had thought about it long and hard, they said, and all in all the best way round it was to issue me with an ID showing that I was Lithuanian, and therefore a citizen of the Soviet Union. When I protested they said there was no alternative and that was that. Therefore I was forced to accept citizenship of the Soviet Union because I could not produce proof that I was born at Tannenwalde/Schlossberg in East Prussia and was a naturalised German. It was a terrible thing for me. Finally I had become officially one of them.

Actually a trap was being prepared, from which it was not going to be so easy to escape. How was I to obtain a copy of my original birth certificate from Schlossberg in the East Prussia border region? In all probability the registry office with all its files had been destroyed at the end of the war. I had found the village of Fichtenhöhe completely gutted when I had visited in 1945. (I did not know then that Richard Schiller, bürgermeister of Fichtenhöhe, had saved all the registry documents, which were now in the safekeeping of his son Georg at Bremen.)

An officer of the KGB came for me. I was to be interrogated at Irkutsk in the administration centre of Colonel-General Miroshnitshenko. They wanted to know the circumstances surrounding the events at Jastrzebiec on 15 November 1944 – my confirmed claims eighty-nine to ninety-two. As Schveitsov led me into the building there was a scramble. Everybody wanted to see the notorious, dangerous Nazi sniper who had lived for many years beneath their very noses, and who had been acquitted by the Supreme War Tribunal, there being no evidence of his having committed any war crimes as a sniper against unarmed personnel. I might easily have been shot on any number of occasions at the front myself, but I had been luckier, faster and more accurate than my opponents. In the event Miroshnitshenko did not call me as a witness to the inquiry. He had other plans for me now that I was a Soviet citizen. He wanted me to spy for Russia. I could have an officer's rank if I would work in West Germany and expiate my guilt by carrying out espionage missions.

I was adamant in rejecting this idea: I could never be a traitor to the comrades who had laid down their lives for me, nor to my German homeland. He retorted that in that case I should abandon hope of ever seeing Germany again. I had no right to a real life: I could only expiate my guilt by a life of servitude to work. I would remain in banishment under the auspices of the KGB. I would have to obey all their instructions. He said, 'A pity, you will regret being alive. We will grant permission to many to leave Soviet territory, but never to you!' and he was as good as his word. I told him I should be satisfied with what I earnt through honest toil. I saw the files they had obtained from the captured German archives. The had done its job well: I had to sign an undertaking never to reveal who I really was and that I would not take part in any propaganda against the Soviet state or take part in any anti-state activity. With that I was allowed to go. I went with mixed feelings – it made me shudder to think that I was to be under the control of these swine for the rest of my life and would have no right ever to go home. But I could never be a traitor to Germany.

I returned to Shiegalva after seeing Toni and Vitautus at the Oblast hospital. It was October 1956. Soon Toni also returned, leaving the boy in the hospital – he was in good hands, for her daughter Grashina was a trainee nurse there; she helped us all she could. On 1 November 1956 I started sawing wood again in the taiga. In a single week, up to my waist in snow, I cut six cubic metres of wood.

When I was still living in Rudovka, I wrote on a number of occasions to Eastern Germany, where I thought my sister Ida was living at Niederdorf in the Erzgebirge near Chemnitz. After her husband had been released from captivity as a PoW, she had moved to Dortmund and none of my letters had reached her. By chance my niece Irmgard, her daughter, was visting Niederdorf when one of my letters arrived, and it was handed to her. It was the first news they had of me in ten years. I received a reply with news of my mother's death in 1949.

I wrote to Erika Lenz and received a reply, and to the old address in Chicago of my grandmother on my father's side. Her last visit to Germany to see her son had been in 1929. A girl of common birth, my father was the outcome of her relationship with a member of the nobility. On the occasion of her last visit, she had given my father some documents, a gold watch bearing a heraldic shield engraved on the lid, and a signet ring with the same device. My father had hurled them all into the fire in a rage. Grandmother cried, but father shouted: 'Better if they had killed me at birth, rather than let me live like this, a man without education, no schooling, and for my signature three crosses.' Today I can understand his pain. He had grown up under very unfavourable circumstances. My letter to his mother, my grandmother, came back 'Addressee deceased'.

# 8

## *Down the Pit: Sherenkov 1957–1971*

After four months we received permission to move house to the outskirts of Irkutsk. As Toni was still subordinated to the commandant at Shiegalva, at the end of March 1957 we settled at Sherenkov, about 125 kilometres outside Irkutsk. On 1 April 1957 I began work as a coal miner. The mining district was called Sherembas. It had more than thirty abandoned pits that had lost the state money. All eastern Siberia was supplied with coal from Sherenkov. It was a filthy town. Eveything was coal-heated. When it was cold in winter and the temperature fell below -40°C a dense fog settled over the town, making it difficult to breathe. It was a place full of criminals of all nationalities, most of whom had served their term in a forced-labour camp but still had to complete their period of banishment – the Tartars, for example. The Volga Germans had no right to return at all, since they had no home. Many coal miners were former Red Army men who had been captured by the Germans and were later 'liberated'. However, they exchanged one PoW camp for something much worse, for now they were in the realm of the Red Terror as traitors to the Russian homeland for having laid down their weapons. Deprived of all rights, they were not allowed to return to their families, but banished forever.

I became a coal miner and was accepted as a safety worker. I knew only the taiga and had never been in a coal mine before. It was very dangerous work in the Russian mines. My partings from Antoniena at the beginning of each shift were very intimate affairs because there was no guarantee I would return in one piece. Every day there was the risk of being crushed or buried alive. In my fourteen years' work underground I often escaped death 'by the skin of my teeth' as Schveitso would have said. Luck smiled upon me.

The pits were dangerous because of the pressure on the supports when coal was removed. A weight of 2,000 tonnes would be exerted on every square metre. If the pit props could not hold it, the gallery caved in and buried the miners. We kept an eye out for the rats. If they came running down the gallery, we had to catch them up. It amazed me how much a mine resembled an underground city. The tunnels were often ten kilometres long with many branch workings, just like a city where all roads feed into the main highways. In the mine the galleries all led to a centre where the wagons were lifted and the coal tipped out onto conveyer belts. This went on day and night.

We were given ten days' training before being put to work. A seam consisted of 30 cm coal, followed by a 5-cm layer of hard stone, then 50 cm coal and a layer of white sand from 5 to 15 cm thick. Our individual face was 2.5 metres in length, which might contain a seam between 40 and 80 cm. It was awkward to work because one had to proceed bent over, work in kneeling positions and slide forward on one leg. Water dripped constantly. After an eight-hour shift one would be soaked through despite special suits and gloves. The beds I started work on were 700 metres long. Support material was brought in, and when the seam was exhausted the structure had to be secured so that the new cycle could begin. The coal at Sherembas was of good quality, comparable to the anthracite from Dombass. As an absolute newcomer I had everything to learn. At the beginning when I returned home after a shift I would often fall asleep at the dinner table, spoon in hand, I was so tired. I was still young and healthy and gradually I became accustomed to the work. I had not forgotten how Colonel-General Miroshnitshenko had promised me when I refused to work for the KGB that I would be sorry I lived, but I would rather perform the heaviest and most dangerous work than be a traitor to those who had given their lives for Germany, their homeland.

The criminal elements I mentioned kept the town of Sherenkov and its 150,000 inhabitants in a state of fear. Burglaries, murders and looting were all quite normal occurrences. The police were powerless. After dark few people would venture out. Everyone was afraid. The only time a homeowner would leave the house would be to bar the exterior windows. If a person was attacked on the street there would be no point in his crying for help, for nobody would come. If one noticed that somebody was about to be robbed, one would give no warning or the accomplices would take their revenge later by blinding the person with a razor blade. It was the unwritten law. It would sometimes happen that better-dressed cinema patrons would be intercepted on their way home and be bludgeoned into unconsciousness. When they came to they would find themselves naked from the waist down in some doorway and have to run home naked, except for socks, in temperatures down to -40°C.

These criminals were mostly former Red Army men who had been convicted of rampages in the Russian occupation zones of eastern Europe. They were not interested in work and preferred a life of crime. They were nicknamed 'parasites', for they had lived on others in the forced-labour camps. It went on with the knowledge of the camp commanders, who would do nothing to prevent it. The proceeds of theft would be shared with the camp guards. The whole point of these camps was to crush humanity ruthlessly underfoot. In the columns, as they were marched out to work, the rule was: 'If you make a step out of line to right or left, this is an escape attempt and you will be shot without warning.' They would announce gleefully beforehand that somebody was going to be shot today. Everything was planned to inculcate fear and terror. The parasites, murderers and rogues terrorised the political prisoners in particular.

Once released from the camp these men formed or joined criminal groups and terrorised the town, murdering, plundering and robbing. They allied to various Russian mafia groups such as 'Black Cat'. Sometimes they would be unable to agree amongst themselves on the division of territory, and bloodshed would result. They were wild beasts and ended their lives as such. The boss received the lion's share of the booty; the rest was split amongst themselves for drink and gambling. Whoever was wiped out in a gambling game had to kill an innocent victim. This was the unwritten law.

One night Toni sent me to the food shop, where I joined a long queue. Others lined up behind me. Two men entered and asked who was last in the queue. It was a girl. One of them said, 'Sorry, but I lost your life in a card game,' drew a dagger from his sleeve and stabbed her. I was within a few metres of the incident. At once there was panic. The assassins left as unobtrusively as they had entered. Who would risk his life to stop them?

One day at the mine our wage was paid out late. It was winter and fell dark early. I was in the queue waiting for payment. As I drew my wage I felt somebody making a sign at my back. I went home with colleagues, but I lived further on than all the rest of them and had to pass the entrances to the barracks. In front of the exit was a gate. I sensed that I was being trailed by two men who were catching up with me fast. Ahead of me I also saw two men who appeared to be drunks. I did not wish to tangle with the latter and stood aside to let them pass. Suddenly they straightened up and confronted me as the other two closed from behind. I was alone and knew that nobody would come to my assistance, no matter how loud I shouted. It was obvious that the objective was my wages. I was a young man and physically strong. One drew a dagger and told me to hand over the money. No sooner were the words out of his mouth than I hit him in the face, breaking his front teeth. The other went for me with an iron bar, but I ducked and put my steel-capped boot in his face. He collapsed at once. The third had drawn a Walther pistol but proved ineffective with it and I smashed the face of the fourth so badly that he fell in the snow and lay still. With all four lying on the ground and 'hors de combat', I collected the pistol, two daggers and the iron bar and proceeded on my way. At the gate before the exit were four more accomplices who had seen everything. I took the safety off the pistol, checked it was loaded and strode rapidly towards them. I think I would probably have shot them down but they ran as soon as they saw I was familiar with the pistol and had released the safety catch.

Antoniena was waiting anxiously for me because she knew that today was payday. When I told her what had happened she was horrified. She cried with fear, being convinced that they would seek retribution and kill me.

Next day I went to the police to report the details and to hand in the weapons. The police captain warned me to be cautious: my life was in danger, the men would wait for the opportunity to murder me. I asked if I would be put on trial in the event there was a fight and I killed someone. He replied, 'If you kill one, keep on doing it!' The upshot was that nobody would stand trial for having defended himself.

I received a threat – when I worked the second shift next week and went home at three in the morning they would be in wait and kill me. Now I had a bad feeling. Toni cried and said I should remain at the mine and come home when it was light. I did this the first night but grew tired of waiting and left at four. All eight of them were waiting at the gate for me. I went forward boldly to face them and see what transpired. They stepped aside. One said, 'You are a brave man. We know you, have made your acquaintance. You have nothing more to fear from us.' They gave me their word of honour and let me pass. In all the years I continued to live in Sherenko they never attacked me again, even when I passed close to them.

Gradually I grew familiar with working in the pits, and to its great dangers. There were many accidents, practically every day. When the sirens howled and the reserve team rushed to our mine, everybody would know that there had been an accident, usually a tunnel collapse. All the families would then come running to find out about their men. In the fourteen years I worked there, until 1 June 1971, more than twenty-eight lost their lives in our division, mostly due to collapsed galleries.

Our brigade was multi-national: Russians, Ukrainians, Germans, Tartars, Azerbaijanis and a Gypsy from Moldavia. Our foreman in charge of safety work with pit props and pillars was a Lithuanian, Cuselius. He arranged it so that I joined his team. During the war women also carried out the safety job. Coal was important: all transport in eastern Siberia depended on the railway locomotives having enough coal. Coal mining was a reserved occupation during the war but the miners had to work twelve-hour shifts. Each emergency exit had ten ladders, with a barred gate at the top to prevent people escaping. The only men permitted to use the lift to exit were those in possession of a docket signed by the foreman to the effect that the man had fulfilled his daily quota. It was heavy work, with poor food. All decent food, so they had said, was for the fighting troops. Anyone who objected was called to the chief engineer's office and received a beating with a rubber-coated cosh while the party secretary and the mine director looked on. There were no protests: it was either the cosh or the front line.

The pit props had to be at least twenty-five centimetres long, half dry and green. They were unloaded from special wagons at the access tunnel. Since water dripped constantly from the ceiling the wood got heavier. Digging out 800 tonnes of coal required enough wood to build an eight-roomed Siberian house. The deeper the coal bed, the greater the pressure on the supports. Sandstone was softer and the pillars would bore into the gallery ceiling under the weight. It was heavy, responsible and dangerous work. Often nothing could be done to prevent a collapse and the tunnel would cave in.

We had reinforced the supports along a face. Water was still dripping from the ceiling when we finished. The supports could not hold the weight: cracking and breaking, they bored into the soft sandstone. We worked desperately to prevent the entire tunnel collapsing, but then it cracked again and buried everyone. We had seen the rats running out in panic beforehand. You never saw a rat trapped in a fall – they sensed the danger and ran. It would have been prudent to have gone hotfoot after the rats, for then we would not have been buried. I lost consciousness briefly, but I was lucky, for a large fall of sandstone was still held by the props. I had been forced against the gallery wall and then buried, unable to move. There was little air, and it was running out. I had to lie quiet and not panic. I heard the rescue team coming and I cried out only when they were near. They heard and worked towards me. I lost consciousness again and must have been close to suffocation. They found me alive but my four companions died. A doctor gave me artificial respiration and got my heart working again. I regained consciousness later.

When the sirens howled and the rescue teams raced to our No 3 mine everybody already knew it was a cave-in. All the women came and waited anxiously for news of their men. Toni came and cried, but then she was told I had been found alive and was being dug out from the rubble. I was taken to hospital but released next day.

All my applications to travel were rejected, and I had to remain in the Soviet paradise. They would not allow me to leave the Soviet Union and get back to Germany. Thus it was more of the same at Sherenkov. I kept working at the mine because I could not earn a similar wage elsewhere. My son was still in the children's tuberculosis hospital at Irkutsk. He was now six and still in plaster. Toni and I used to visit him often.

Most workers had beaten all the odds to get here, having survived a forced-labour camp to find themselves still under sentence of banishment. They were not allowed home. Soviet soldiers who had surrendered to the Germans were considered traitors and had life banishment. It was the Bolshevik point of view that they were supposed to fight and not put their hands up. Thus Stalin had millions of dead Russians to add to his personal account.

During the war, men in the forced-labour camps had been sent to punishment battalions at the front, which were no bed of roses – they were forced to fight at the worst hotspots in the front line 'to prove themselves'. Most perished in the German defensive fire. To encourage them to go forward, NKVD units with Bolshevik commissars and officers would shoot a few in the back if any reluctance was evident. They had no choice but to be shot in the back by the NKVD or in the front by the Germans. A human life had no value in the Soviet system.

In the mines we were all equal. Nobody ever demanded another's identity or nationality or the reason for his banishment. Every man was judged on his value as a worker and colleague. We looked death in the face hourly. I had gained respect and recognition and had been awarded the name 'Boris Antonevich'.

The Soviet miner was cruelly exploited. For his hard graft he was paid just enough to keep him on the breadline. The fruits of his labours were harvested by others, like lice on his body. The Communist Party and all the party bosses sucked their profit from those who worked with sweat and blood. In the factories and other work ventures throughout the Soviet Union, the party organs controlled everything, receiving their instructions from the central organisation of the Communist Party. All grandiose five-year plans for the communist expansion of industry were achieved on the back of the slaves in the forced-labour camps: achieved from the suffering, misery and blood of many innocent people. The whole country was a giant prison camp from which we hoped one day we might be freed.

I had been working at the coal face. The weather above was very wet and water dripped from the ceiling as though it were raining. We were always soaked through. Pit props floated in the galleries. The ventilation system by the emergency exits blasted ice-cold air into the interior, creating a layer of ice on the coal face. We had to leave the mine by these exits and run three kilometres, soaking wet, in temperatures of forty degrees below, to get to the collective combine. There we stood for another ten to fifteen minutes for our frozen special clothing and rubber boots to thaw out so that we could take them off. Only then did we take a hot shower and warm ourselves up. As a result of this, I fell very ill. Thick suppurative matter formed under my skull and did not discharge through my nose. I was admitted to hospital, where the ENT surgeon poked a thick needle up my nasal cavity to draw off the foreign matter, and then injected honey into the cerebral membrane. I felt a great relief. The surgeon spoke excellent German for a foreigner and was very attentive to me.

Our No 3 mine had 1,300 members, of whom 1,000 worked to produce coal and the other 300 were 'auxiliaries' linked to the Communist Party bureau. A *Komsomol* (young communist) was secretary and received his remuneration without actually doing anything. The party secretary received a monthly salary equivalent to 90 per cent of what the mine director earnt, the workers' union representative 80 per cent and the *Komsomol* secretary of the Communist Youth Union 70 per cent. None of these people did anything useful towards running the mine – they were paid good salaries for painting communist slogans on the walls.

Communist Party members paid 3 per cent of their wages for their regular party subscriptions and 1 per cent to the union representative. This was how the workers were robbed of their earnings. Every worker had to belong to the union as a condition of employment. The union could send workers to a sanatorium if the case demanded, and the representative was available to the mine administration to give advice on all matters, although this would not include human rights petitions.

All offices were crammed with technical persons – engineers – from all kinds of sub-sections. It was alleged that they had so much work they could hardly cope. In reality it was simply a bureaucracy in which they sat on the coal produced by the miners and sucked their blood. All these bureaucrats were party members, often locked in secret sessions. The party secretary prepared everything down to the smallest detail. All questions and answers were worked out and then aired at public meetings. Since everything was already decided, the chairman had his list of speakers ready in advance. Here we had 'democracy in action' and 'free democratic elections' by which the people were gagged and cheated.

# 9

## *I Keep Agitating for my Exit Visa*

I corresponded with my sister Ida in Dortmund and former German Red Cross nurse Erika Lenz, who had some of my papers and all my war decorations. In 1958, a year after I started work in the pits, I was granted twenty-four days' leave for the first time since I had been in the Soviet Union, and I travelled to Lithuania to visit my father. I wanted to get hold of personal papers relating to my service with the Wehrmacht, which my mother had preserved for me. She had always carried them with her, believing that the day would eventually come when I should be able to make use of them. It was far too dangerous for me to keep them at that time and so I had stuffed them in a bottle, hermetically sealed the stopper to keep the contents dry and buried it secretly. My intention was to retrieve it eventually and take it to the West German embassy in Moscow.

Now I did so. I took the train back to Russia in December 1958 and saw a Herr Bock at our embassy in Moscow and gave him my Wehrmacht papers. They brought me tea and a lady asked if it was very cold in Siberia. I told her I went colder at the thought of having to go back there. She assured me that everything would be done to obtain an exit visa for my family and me. Herr Bock asked if I were ill, because I looked so pale. I replied, 'You would be pale if you knew you had to travel back out to eastern Siberia in the far east and never know if you will survive each work shift!' He promised to do everything possible to get me out. 'You are a German citizen and nobody has the right to detain you any longer. We will send a note to the Soviet Foreign Ministry to have you released.' I did not have a lot of confidence that this would do much good. Herr Bock gave me a new suit, pullover, shoes and thirty new roubles. He said I should change in the embassy and put nothing in my pack for they would probably arrest me outside. The Soviets would search anything I brought out and be very unpleasant. I was poor, however, lacked clothing and had to preserve what I had, so I took the whole lot with me. After a lady staff member at the embassy came to sympathise and kiss me farewell, I finally forced myself to leave the West German embassy.

A hundred metres outside I was stopped by Soviet security men who showed me their identity cards and took me to their offices for a search. They recorded the numbers of the thirty bank notes, gave me a brief interrogation and released me. Upon my return to Sherenkov I was summoned before Colonel Dirkutsh, who questioned me. He wanted to know with whom I had spoken at the West German embassy and what they had asked me. I told him they wanted to know my place of birth, if I were a German national, in what unit of the Wehrmacht I had served, where I had seen action and how I had finished up in Siberia. He asked why I had been given the thirty roubles. I said I thought it must have been for me to buy food. He waved me away, and I returned to work. Now I waited, counting the days and months, yearning for the happy day when I could return to Germany my homeland. I did not know it then, but I had only thirty-two more years to wait!

I wrote screeds about this longing in my diaries. Toni warned me that I would be discredited if they were found. The West German embassy wrote confirming that I was born at Tannenwalde/Schlossberg in East Prussia, and not Lithuania. At my request the family register was sent to me. The embassy also sent a note to the Soviet Foreign Ministry asking for steps to be taken to guarantee the exit from the Soviet Union for myself and my family. I was recommended to make an application for an exit visa to the relevant authorities, which I did.

The Soviets always found a reason to turn down my applications. Now they wanted my old German ID document or a certificate issued at Fichtenhöhe, a town that no longer existed. So I could not produce the certificate, not the original birth certificate they also asked for. All I received instead was a letter to the effect that no archives were stored in the central depository in Berlin or at the Schillfelde registry, these having been destroyed in fighting at the end of the war. The German Foreign Office was also taking an interest in my case and so I did not give up hope entirely. Major Seitsko of the KGB told me more than once that I was wasting my time making applications to leave. 'Even if they send a hundred notes, you will remain in our hands. Only we decide if you are allowed to go!'

Before my father died, he asked me to have him buried in a grave beside my mother. I promised that I would see to this. One day I received a telegram that my father had died on 6 March 1960 and had been interred. I requested leave, which was granted. Without it I could not have left Sherenkov.

My father had been buried at Leketschai cemetery. The grave of my mother, who had died on 1 January 1949, was also there. I had taken the four volumes of diaries that I had written about East Prussia, hoping to hand them in at the West German embassy as part of my campaign to obtain my exit visa. On the train a day short of Moscow I left my belongings unattended on my seat for a call of nature. When I returned I found that the KGB had ransacked my things and taken my diaries. Nobody in the carriage had seen anything. I was annoyed to have lost the diaries, and at myself for not having listened to Toni. The KGB was aware that I was interested in the life stories of other banishees; most of them were former members of the Waffen-SS. I do not know who the informant was, if there was one. I suppose anybody might have seen me writing prodigiously at the window of our house. Now all my work had gone.

In Moscow I took the metro from Belarus Station. I had eight hours to kill before my train left for Vilnius in Lithuania, and I made for the West German embassy. I was carrying a small case – the lock was broken and the left-luggage would not accept it. On B-Grusinskaya Street a car pulled up beside me and two men jumped out. 'You, citizen, stole the bag of a lady on Belarus Station. Get in the car at once while we investigate!' When I refused they showed me their badges. They were a Colonel and Major of the KGB. Soon we arrived at their palatial HQ at 36 Kusniszova Street. Two guards with white gloves and Kalashnikovs guarded the portals. I was led into an office for interrogation.

'Where were you going?'
'To the West German embassy.'
'Had you arranged to meet somebody there?'
'No.'

'Why were you going there?'

'I wanted to ask what I could do to obtain an exit visa.'

'Are you unaware that you are a citizen of the USSR?'

'I cannot read Russian. I am a German.'

A side door opened and the head of the KGB, Andropov, came in. The other two snapped to attention and made their report, after which he dismissed them. We were alone together.

'You should be proud to be a citizen of today's Soviet Union.' I replied that I could not feel about it the same way as he did – the homeland of one's birth and where one grew up were dear to everybody, but it was not necessarily the country that fate had forced one to adopt. He asked what war decorations I had been awarded. I told him and said, 'Why did your soldiers at the front receive medals?'

'For fighting bravely for the motherland.'

'I was brought up to love my German homeland and fatherland and die for it if necessary.'

'Do you not find it difficult to square it with your conscience that you killed so many Russian soldiers and officers?'

'No, I was fighting armed men. And at the front you would never have taken me alive. My last bullet was for myself.'

He was very interested in my technical abilities. I told him that I had grown up on the German side of the border with Lithuania and often crossed the frontier near the border guards to establish their actual positions.

Now he said he had a proposition. I could leave Siberia with 25,000 roubles in my pocket and settle anywhere I chose in the Soviet empire: Moscow or Vilnius if I liked. All I had to do was declare before foreign press correspondents that I was in the Soviet Union voluntarily and no longer wanted an exit visa since I had decided to settle down here. I declined at once, saying that I could not be bought. To that he made the standard reply that I had no right to live and ought to be shot or put into solitary confinement in a forced-labour camp in order to atone for my guilt of killing so many Russian officers and men. He also wanted to know how many I thought the total was. I replied that in the war at the front, the man who survived was the one who was luckier, and shot more accurately than the other side's snipers. I had not been invulnerable, but shot more accurately than those whose bullets whistled close by me. I asked him why I was not being allowed to leave the Soviet Union. He said, 'You are a well-known personality. You have lived here all this time. We cannot let you go because you have seen everything with your own eyes and been in close contact with our people. You could engage in anti-Soviet propaganda for radio or television.' He warned me that there were people in Germany at his disposal to liquidate me. Even there I would not be safe from them. The East German police would maintain a permanent watch on me. They would not trust me because I was contaminated ideologically. I should not be prey to empty illusions. In conclusion he requested me not to go to the West German embassy when I returned from Lithuania. He stood up, offered me his hand and said that I was a good worker, a sound, upright person. Then he released me. To my great surprise he gave orders for me to be taken to Belerenske Station, where I was put aboard the train for Lithuania. I had been prepared for the worst – incarceration in their prisons at Butirka or Lenakam.

In Vilnius I visited Toni's elder son and next day went to Kauen. The police kept tabs on me and kept checking with the relevant authorities but left me in peace. As my father had been in the ground for over a week I had to apply to the administrator of Leketschai to exhume the body, and I was allowed to reinter the coffin alongside that of my mother. Thus I fulfilled his last wish.

In the barn of a certain house I dug up various personal papers and 8,000 Reichsmark. The money was worthless now, and I took it for Vitautus to play with. My parents had worked hard to save it in the hope of buying a small farm, but the outcome of the war had brought all these ideas to nought.

Back with Antoniena I resumed work down the pits. Early one morning in June 1967 on my way to the mine a lorry cut me up. I threw myself from my motor-cycle but fell heavily. This accident could have killed me. Another lorry stopped and took me to hospital. Meanwhile, the Soviets continued to reject all my requests for an exit visa.

# 10

## *Released from Banishment but not the Soviet Empire*

In 1969 Antoniena was released from banishment and allowed to return to Lithuania. She moved in with her elder son in Vilnius. A condition of her release was that she signed a disclaimer of ownership to the farm property. I remained in eastern Siberia. In 1970 I visited Toni while in Vilnius and applied to join her there. I was told I would have to marry her to obtain permission, and after twenty-four years living together we married at Marijampole on 18 August 1970. This enabled our son Vitautus, reading mathematics and physics at Vilnius, to use my surname. Despite the marriage, no permission was forthcoming, and I had to return to Sherenkov. I took leave of my wife and son with a heavy heart. Unlike 1949, when a cattle truck had conveyed me across the vast expanses of Russia, I sat at the window of a passenger train and remembered 25 March 1949, the day of our banishment, and the unhappy people crying and praying. Most of them died miserably in Siberia.

Finally in 1971, while I was still working in the coal mine, Toni received approval from the Soviet Interior Ministry for me to relocate to Vilnius with her. After twenty-two years I abandoned Siberia forever to join my wife. In Vilnius I could find no work at first: the KGB watched both me and our flat. Finally I found employment as an electro-gas welder in a factory making reinforced concrete. I was made foreman, and kept the technology functioning, since many of the Lithuanians were alcoholics and so unable to keep pace. On my fiftieth birthday on 14 May 1974 I applied for my miner's pension.

In Lithuania I was homesick and nostalgic for my old homeland. The feeling could not be suppressed – the urge to revisit Fichtenhöhe could not be resisted. I knew of course that there was nothing there, everything had been destroyed and all vestiges of German life expelled. After the war the Soviets turned the region into a tank plain and staged great mock battles involving aircraft, artillery and tanks.

Where once a peaceable folk worked on the village farms – East Prussia was the bread basket of the German Reich and fed millions – everything in 1974 stood empty, reduced to rubble, a ravaged desert. The farms, hamlets and villages not destroyed in the war became bombing targets for the Soviet Air Force. Toni tried to dissuade me from going: I could be arrested. What would she do without me? Nevertheless I would not be deterred and took three days' leave. Crossing the bridge at Kuchirch Nammestas I entered East Prussia. The border guards checked my ID and waved me across.

I reached the location where Schirwindt had existed. The town had vanished. Where the church had been was level ground; grass grew between the lumps of masonry. There was a bust of Lenin, and one cow at pasture. It looked as though some terrible natural disaster had hit it. Undergrowth had reclaimed the road to Fichtenhöhe. I met a man who had worked on a farm at Fichtenhöhe before the war; we recognised each other. His advice was to take the bus to Turshenai in Lithuania. Fichtenhöhe lay opposite, just across the Scheschuppe. We walked back together. All that remained of Schirwindt was a cobbled street lined with the same old trees that led to the Nammestas bridge. We came shopping here before the war, and our family and relations used to cross into Nammestas annually for the church festivals.

There was no bus until the morning and so I walked the twelve kilometres to Turshenai, which took me a couple of hours. The Scheschuppe followed its old course from Memel. The level was too high to wade to Fichtenhöhe – I had to wait for morning. At Turshenai an old lady recognised me and put me up for the night. Next morning her son took me to where I could ford the river. There was a strong current running, but only waist high. I put my clothing on my head to keep it dry and dressed on the other side. Some Russians soldiers asked me if there was any vodka in Turshenai; they stripped down and waded across to find some.

They were stationed with a work battalion near Arno Braemer's farmhouse, working on some kind of rocket.

I ran up the bank. Here on the river shore in spring the first wood anemones and violets bloomed. I plucked some and ascended the slope to where Moosbach had been. It was now wild bush. Heading towards Fichtenhöhe I found only abandoned fields – a Sovietised wilderness. Where the beautiful path had lain only the towering fir trees had survived, along with the remnants of a German machine-gun nest near the river. The park had much wild undergrowth and brush. Arno Braemer's farm had been reduced to a mass of rubble with a cellar. All the buildings had disappeared but the foundations remained. I found where my parents' house had stood: now a pile of broken brickwork.

On the way to Fichtenhöhe I picked some forget-me-nots in the graveyard. The grave edges had been removed although some crosses still stood. Trees and scrub grew everywhere. I found the sunken road to the Scheschuppe, keeping a sharp lookout on all sides. Like a thief I crept though this region of East Prussia – my homeland – in 1974 controlled by Soviet occupiers, from the 1990s onwards Polish territory. I undressed, put my trousers and shoes on my head and waded the river back to Lithuania. So ended my visit to my native land. This had once been my home, and in my heart it will always be so.

Work at the reinforced-concrete factory went on, and the years slipped by. My sister Ida died in the 1980s in Dortmund. In the spring of 1990 I was taken ill and advised to give up work. Work kept me going, and because I could not leave Antoniena alone too long I worked alternate day and night shifts. We had a three-room flat, and in 1991 I had a pension of 500 roubles. That was our only income. My son now lived in Kedainius, 150 kilometres away. I had no option as I saw it but to continue to work.

A new era arrived. The Bolshevik epoch of the Soviet Union finally came to its end. As its borders fell I was finally free, and rehabilitated. In 1991, the Lithuanian Parliament declared the country's independence. After the communist curse was lifted, the Lithuanian newspapers discovered me. They printed long articles about the mysterious Wehrmacht sniper. As late as the year 2000, they were still writing about my life and my service at the front. I came to the attention of the newly constituted Lithuanian Army and at Vilnius delivered to young soldiers a number of lectures on my experiences as a sniper. I also addressed military cadets at the War Academy in Vilnius.

# 11

## *My German Nationality Restored*

My niece Irmgard, Ida's daughter, sent a letter inviting Vitautus and myself to visit her in Germany. This letter was enough to obtain a German entry visa, and finally after forty-five years' absence I re-trod German soil on 12 May 1990. I met my niece and Erika Regli-Lenz, now living in Andermatt, Switzerland, who also came to our joyful reunion.

We went to the German authorities to enquire about my citizenship. They did not seem to grasp the fact that I was not an old Lithuanian applying to be German, but a naturalised German whose papers had been lost by myself and the state due to the Second World War. They said I would have to reside in a resettlement camp, perhaps for years, before acceptance. Weighed down with presents, a week later I returned to Lithuania to begin the struggle to reconfirm my German nationality. Eventually I obtained a certificate of German citizenship and finally in 1994 my German passport. In 1995 the German Parliamentary Secretary of State and Bundestag Deputy, Gertrud Dempwolf, visited me in Vilnius to provide further help.

Toni died shortly afterwards. She was in her nineties by then. I had cared for her to the last. Later I married my present wife, Lydia.

At last the day came when I could leave Lithuania. On the morning of 29 January 1997 I arrived in Berlin via Danzig. After fifty-two years I was home again in Germany.

~

*German Publisher's Note*

After Bruno Sutkus had resettled in Germany in 1997, on 20 January 1998 the Central Compensation Office in Bavaria refused his request for financial assistance to reintegrate. That is the recognition shown in modern Germany towards those of its soldiers who fought and bled for the Germany of the past.

~

# Index

*Page numbers in italics represent illustrations*

~

Other books on the Second World War published by Frontline
include:

*AT ROMMEL'S SIDE*
The Lost Letters of Hans-Joachim Schraepler
Edited by Hans-Albrecht Schraepler
Introduction by Dennis Showalter
ISBN 978-1-84832-538-8

*CHURCHILL'S UNDERGROUND ARMY*
A History of the Auxiliary Units in World War II
John Warwicker
Foreword by Lord Ironside
ISBN 978-1-84832-515-9

*COUNTDOWN TO VALKYRIE*
The July Plot to Assassinate Hitler
Nigel Jones
Afterword with Count Berthold Schenk von Stauffenberg
ISBN 978-1-84832-508-1

*THE DEVIL'S WORKSHOP*
A Memoir of the Nazi Counterfeiting Operation
Adolf Burger
ISBN 978-1-84832-523-4

*ESCAPE FROM THE THIRD REICH*
Folke Bernadotte and the White Buses
Sune Persson
Preface by Brian Urquhart
ISBN 978-1-84832-556-2

*THE GESTAPO*
A History of Horror
Jacques Delarue
ISBN 978-1-84832-502-9

*HE WAS MY CHIEF*
The Memoirs of Adolf Hitler's Secretary
Christa Schroeder
Introduction by Roger Moorhouse
ISBN 978-1-84832-536-4

*HITLER'S ROCKETS*
The Story of the V-2s
Norman Longmate
ISBN 978-1-84832-546-3

*I WAS HITLER'S CHAUFFEUR*
The Memoirs of Erich Kempka
Erich Kempka
Introduction by Roger Moorhouse
ISBN 978-1-4832-550-0
Publication 2010

*LAST DAYS OF THE LUFTWAFFE*
German Luftwaffe Combat Units 1944-1945
Manfred Griehl
ISBN 978-1-84832-511-1

*LAST DAYS OF THE REICH*
The Diary of Count Folke Bernadotte, October 1944–May 1945
Count Folke Bernadotte
Introduction by Sune Persson
ISBN 978-1-84832-522-7

*THE MEN WHO TRIED TO KILL HITLER*
The Attempt on Hitler's Life in July 1944
Heinrich Fraenkel and Roger Manvell
Foreword by Roger Moorhouse
ISBN 978-1-84832-509-8

*NO CLOAK NO DAGGER*
Allied Spycraft in Occupied France
Benjamin Cowburn
Introduction by M. R. D. Foot
Foreword by Sebastian Faulks
ISBN 978-1-84832-543-2

*REPORT ON EXPERIENCE*
A Memoir of the Allies' War
John Mulgan
Introduction by M. R. D. Foot
Foreword by Richard Mulgan
ISBN 978-1-84832-554-8

*TAPPING HITLER'S GENERALS*
Transcripts of Secret Conversations, 1942–1945
Sönke Neitzel
Foreword by Ian Kershaw
ISBN 978-1-84415-705-1

*THE VENLO INCIDENT*
How the Nazis Fooled Britain
Captain Sigismund Payne-Best
Introduction by Nigel Jones
ISBN 978-1-84832-558-6

*WITH HITLER TO THE END*
The Memoirs of Adolf Hitler's Valet
Heinz Linge
Introduction by Roger Moorhouse
ISBN 978-1-84832-544-9

For more information on our books, please visit
www.frontline-books.com.
You can write to us at info@frontline-books.com or
47 Church Street, Barnsley, S. Yorkshire, S70 2AS